The Surgeon of Crowthorne

SIMON WINCHESTER

Level 5

Retold by Michael Dean
Series Editors: Andy Hopkins and Jocelyn Potter

Pearson Education Limited
Edinburgh Gate, Harlow,
Essex CM20 2JE, England
and Associated Companies throughout the world.

ISBN 0 582 43565 X

First published by Viking 1998
Published by Penguin Books 2001

Original copyright © Simon Winchester 1998
Text copyright © Penguin Books 2001

Typeset by Ferdinand Pageworks, London
Set in 11/14pt Bembo
Printed in Spain by Mateu Cromo, S. A. Pinto (Madrid)

Published by Pearson Education Limited in association with
Penguin Books Ltd, both companies being subsidiaries of Pearson Plc

Contents

For George Merrett of Lambeth

Introduction

'I, sir, am Dr James Murray,' he said in his beautiful voice with the Scottish accent. *'I am the editor of the* New English Dictionary. *And you, sir, must be Dr William Minor, a contributor for the last seventeen years. I am very happy to meet you at last.'*

There was a short silence. Then the other man replied, *'I am sorry, sir, but I am not your contributor, Dr Minor. I am the Governor of Broadmoor Asylum for the Criminally Insane. Dr Minor is an American, and he has been here for some time. He murdered a man. He is quite insane.'*

The Surgeon of Crowthorne is the true story of Dr James Murray and Dr William Minor. In some ways they were similar. They looked, strangely, almost exactly the same. They both worked on the *Oxford English Dictionary*. But in other ways they were very different. James Murray was Scottish and lived a happy, quiet life with his family. William Chester Minor was American, fought in the American Civil War, murdered a man and went mad. He lived the most unhappy life you are ever likely to read about.

Simon Winchester is a well-known journalist and writer. He was born in England but has lived in Africa, India and Asia and now lives in New York. Some of his other books are: *Prison Diary, Argentina,* the story of three months in prison accused of being a spy during the Falklands War, and *The River at the Centre of the World – A Journey Up the Yangtze and Back in Chinese Time,* which is also published by Penguin.

Chapter 1   Dr Murray's First Meeting with Dr Minor

There is a story about the first meeting of Dr James Murray, the editor of the great *Oxford English Dictionary*, and Dr William C. Minor, an important contributor.

It is said that, in 1896, Dr Murray wrote to Dr Minor. His letter, according to the story, read like this:

'You and I have now been writing to each other for seventeen years and it is a sad fact that we have never met. Perhaps you have never been able to travel; maybe it has been too expensive. But although it is difficult for me to leave my editorial work for even one day, I have wanted to meet you for a long time. Would it therefore be possible for me to visit you? If this is convenient, perhaps you could suggest a day and a train, and I will tell you the time of my expected arrival.'

Minor replied immediately, saying that he would of course be very pleased to see the editor. He was sorry that it had not been possible for him to travel to Oxford, and he suggested several possible trains from those listed in *Bradshaw's Railway Guide*. His address, as Murray already knew after years of correspondence, was Broadmoor, Crowthorne, Berkshire.

Murray chose a November Wednesday and a train that, with a change in Reading, would arrive at Crowthorne Railway Station a short time after lunch.

On that November Wednesday, Murray rode his old three-wheeled bicycle down the Banbury Road in Oxford. His long, white beard blew over his shoulder in the cold wind as he cycled past the Randolph Hotel, the Ashmolean Museum and Worcester College to Oxford Station.

The train journey took just a little over an hour. It was a

pleasant surprise, when he arrived at Crowthorne, to find a coach and horses waiting for him. He had always thought Minor must be a man who had a lot of free time for reading. But now it seemed that he might be wealthy as well. Wealthy enough to own a coach pulled by four horses.

The horses pulled Murray through narrow streets and a countryside wet with fog. Crowthorne village was a pretty little place, quiet, with plenty of trees and just a few tiny houses.

Broadmoor was a little apart from the village. As the horses pulled the coach towards the great house, there were fewer houses and more trees. They stopped in front of enormous gates, which were quickly opened by servants.

Inside, Murray took off the warm coat that had protected him from the cold. A silent servant led him into a large room with a coal fire. On the walls there were paintings of serious-looking men. There was a large desk and, behind it, a well-built man who was obviously important. The servant left and closed the door.

Murray walked towards the great man. The great man stood. Murray held out his hand.

'I, sir, am Dr James Murray,' he said in his beautiful voice with the Scottish accent. 'I am the editor of the *New English Dictionary*. And you, sir, must be Dr William Minor, a contributor for the last seventeen years. I am very happy to meet you at last.'

There was a short silence. Then the other man replied, 'I am sorry, sir, but I am not your contributor, Dr Minor. I am the Governor of Broadmoor Asylum for the Criminally Insane. Dr Minor is an American, and he has been here for some time. He murdered a man. He is quite insane.'

Murray, the story continues, was amazed, but still asked to see Dr Minor. The meeting between the two men who had worked together on the dictionary for so long, and who had corresponded so often, was of great interest to both of them.

The story of this first meeting is, however, a fiction. It was created by an American journalist named Hayden Church, who lived in London for most of the first half of the twentieth century. It first appeared in England in the *Strand* magazine, in September 1915. Church had also written the same story for the *Sunday Star* in Washington DC, in July 1915.

AMERICAN MURDERER HELPED WRITE OXFORD DICTIONARY said the newspaper story.

And that was absolutely true.

◆

In fact, the first contact between Murray and Minor came very soon after work began on the dictionary – probably in 1880 or 1881. 'He was a very good contributor who wrote to me often,' Murray wrote to a friend in Boston. 'By accident I found out that "Broadmoor, Crowthorne, Berkshire" was the address of a large asylum.'

At first Murray thought that Minor must be a doctor, helping the criminally insane. Murray and Minor corresponded only about the dictionary, of course. And Murray was pleased with Minor's work and he was not interested in anything else about him.

But then, some time between 1887 and 1890, Murray had a visitor, an American librarian. Justin Winsor, of Harvard College, told Murray his contributor's story.

So Murray wrote to Minor, and also wrote to the Governor of Broadmoor Asylum, Dr Nicholson. Murray then visited Minor in January 1891 – six years earlier than in the story started by Hayden Church.

Murray had lunch at Broadmoor with Dr Nicholson and Minor, who was a great favourite of Dr Nicholson's children. Murray then had a long talk with Minor in his room – or cell – at the asylum.

Murray thought Minor was 'as sane as myself', a fine man who had read a lot of books, knew a lot about art, and had accepted his life in an asylum. Minor was sad only because he was less useful to the dictionary in the asylum than he would be outside it.

♦

It took more than seventy years to create the twelve books of the *Oxford English Dictionary*. (It was called the *New English Dictionary* until 1933, but after that people used the new initials, *OED*.) Then work started on it again until, in the end, twenty enormous books defined the whole of the English language − a language now used everywhere in the modern world.

English is a large and complicated language, so the *OED* is a large and complicated set of books. It defines more than half a million words. The meanings and uses of each word are shown by quotations from other books. This is still the best way of explaining the different meanings of a single word.

These quotations show how a word has been used differently over the centuries. Most important, perhaps, they also show how and when each word first entered the language.

But this method of producing a dictionary takes a lot of time; many readers are needed to find and list the different uses of a word.

Work on the enormous books of the *OED* began in the 1850s, but it was so slow that the language was changing faster than the dictionary was being written. Other books had to be added to the work that was finally produced, with words defined in new ways. The *OED* is a very expensive set of books to produce and to buy.

But it sells well. It is an important book for any library. It can answer any question about the use of a word in the English language, and it does this with complete confidence. The *OED* has been criticised for this confidence − and for the fact that the dictionary defines offensive words too cautiously.

But despite the criticisms, many people consider the *OED* to be one of the most important books in the world. And as the importance of the English language increases, the *OED* becomes more important too.

This book is the story of the 'father' of the *OED*, the editor Dr James Augustus Henry Murray, and one of the dictionary's most helpful contributors, Dr William Chester Minor. These are the two main characters in this story.

Or you could say that these are the two main 'protagonists' in this story. If you do not know the word *protagonist*, you can look it up in the *OED*. You will find that there are three main meanings of the word. You will find nineteen quotations showing those meanings from, among others, the detective story writer Dorothy L. Sayers and from the plays of the great George Bernard Shaw. You will find that the word was first used by the poet John Dryden in 1671. You will find that the word *protagonist* can be used in the plural, even though Henry Fowler, in his *Modern English Usage (1926)*, said that this use was grammatically wrong.

So we *can* say that there are two protagonists to this story. One of them was a quiet gentleman from Scotland. The other was an insane American murderer.

Chapter 2   A Saturday Night in Lambeth

In 1872, the area of London known as Lambeth Marsh, along the bank of the River Thames, just across from Westminster, was a dark and dangerous place. It was full of narrow streets of poor houses. It was a violent place, with pickpockets and thieves waiting to rob and steal, and no honest man ever admitted to visiting it. This was the London that Charles Dickens wrote about in *Oliver Twist*; his characters Fagin, the pickpocket, and the

5

criminal Bill Sikes would probably have felt quite at home if they had visited Lambeth Marsh.

It was also a place of cheap entertainment, and the sort of area where a man could pay a prostitute to spend the night with him. Lambeth Marsh was just outside London, with its strict laws, and just inside Surrey, where the laws were more relaxed. So when Londoners wanted to see a play that would not be allowed on the stage in London, or to drink strong alcohol, or to pay for a prostitute for the night, they 'went Surreyside', to Lambeth Marsh.

But it was cheap to live in Lambeth Marsh, so as well as the men 'going Surreyside' from London, there were honest working men, like George Merrett.

Merrett lived at 24 Cornwall Cottages, Cornwall Road, and by February 1872 he had worked at the Red Lion Brewery for eight years. The process of making beer involved a fire burning through the day and night. George Merrett was one of the men who kept the fires burning.

Like many young workers in the London of Dickens's time, Merrett and his wife Eliza had come from the country. Both of them had worked on the land, doing boring, back-breaking work, hour after hour, for a tiny amount of money. Then they caught one of the new fast trains to the capital, looking for work and for an improved way of life.

George and Eliza's oldest child, Clare, was born in 1860 at the Merretts' first London home, in the north of the city. By 1867, the family was already too large for their first home and work was difficult to find. So the Merretts moved to Lambeth Marsh. The air was dirty and their house was very small. The toilet was a hole outside the house, shared with many others. But there was also a cheerful good humour, typical of London. We shall never know if the Merretts missed the fields and streams of their previous country life.

By the winter of 1871, George and Eliza had the large family typical of workers who lived in the tiny dark houses of Dickens's London: six children, from Clare, who was nearly twelve years old, to Freddy, who was aged twelve months. And Mrs Merrett was upstairs getting ready to have a seventh baby.

They were a poor family: most families in Lambeth Marsh were poor. The rent had to be paid and there were eight mouths to feed, so there was never enough money. But George had joined a Friendly Society. These Friendly Societies used to be popular across Britain. They offered help to the workers in their old age or when no work could be found, years before the government started helping people.

On the night of 17 February 1872, another worker at the Red Lion Brewery, who was a member of the same Friendly Society, wanted to leave work early. George Merrett exchanged work times with him, agreeing to start work at two in the morning and work for the next eight hours. As arranged, a neighbour knocked on the Merretts' window to wake George up. It was a very cold morning, and he dressed as warmly as a poor man could. He wore a coat that had holes in it and, under that, the kind of jacket that was popular in the 1870s, an old grey shirt, trousers tied at the ankle with string, heavy socks and black boots. The clothes were not clean, but George would be putting coal on a fire for the next eight hours, so he was not very interested in how he appeared.

Eliza remembered George leaving their home: she saw him for the last time under one of the new gas street lights that had just been put up in Lambeth Marsh. Eliza could see his breath in the cold air – or perhaps he was smoking his pipe – as he walked quickly to the end of Cornwall Road, before turning left into Upper Ground and then along to Belvedere Road. The night was clear and full of stars and silent, except for the noise of the trains, which was never-ending in that part of London at that time.

Mrs Merrett was not worried about her husband. George had

started work at two o'clock in the morning many times before, and nothing out of the ordinary had ever happened. He walked to the Red Lion Brewery with the famous red lion above it – it was well known in that part of London, and people were proud to work there. He put coal on the brewery's fires for eight hours, and then he came home.

But that night George Merrett did not arrive at the Red Lion Brewery. As he passed Tenison Street, not very far from the brewery, someone shouted at him and started to chase him, still shouting. Merrett was frightened. This was not an ordinary thief; thieves were silent. Merrett began to run, his boots sliding on the cold street. He looked back and the man was still there, chasing him, shouting angrily. Then, quite amazingly, the man stopped and fired a gun at him.

Criminals did not carry guns in the London of Dickens's time. Guns were expensive, and they were difficult to carry around, to use and to hide. Then, as now, the use of a gun during a crime was thought of as somehow not very British. It was something to be written about, because it was so unusual.

The shot missed, went past Merrett's head and hit the brewery wall. George Merrett tried to run faster. He cried out for help. There was another shot. Perhaps another. And then a final shot that hit the unfortunate Merrett in the neck. He fell heavily onto the pavement, his face down, a pool of blood spreading around him.

By this time the first of the three – or perhaps four – shots had been heard, and although shots were so rare, they had been recognised as shots. The man who heard them was a young policeman named Henry Tarrant.

The clocks had only just struck two, his notes said later; he had been walking slowly past Waterloo Railway Station, in the freezing cold. He had been checking the locks on the shops in the empty streets, at this silent time of the early morning.

When he heard the shots, Tarrant blew his whistle to attract the attention of other policemen, and began to run. He was certain the sounds had come from Belvedere Road. Within seconds he had raced through the dark, narrow streets and arrived there.

Another policeman, named Henry Burton, had heard the whistle and so had a third, William Ward, and they all ran towards Belvedere Road. According to Burton's notes, he found Tarrant, who was holding a man by the arm. 'Quick,' shouted Tarrant. 'Go down the road – a man has been shot!' Burton and Ward ran along Belvedere Road, and within seconds found the unmoving body of a dying man. They knelt down in the road and tried to help him. But the dying man could not be helped, as the newspapers who later reported 'The Lambeth Marsh Tragedy' told their readers.

The policemen took him to St Thomas's Hospital, which was a little further along Belvedere Road. The doctors examined George Merrett, and tried to close the large wound in his neck. But two bullets had gone into his neck and he had bled to death.

◆

Within minutes of the crime, the man who had committed it was being held by Henry Tarrant. The man was tall and well dressed, and Henry Tarrant thought that he had been in the army. He looked like an army man; he stood with his head high and his back straight. He had a gun in his right hand and there was smoke coming out of it. He did not try to run away but stood silently as the policeman approached.

'Who fired a gun?' asked the policeman.

'I did,' said the man and held up the gun.

Tarrrant took it from him. 'Who did you fire at?' he asked.

The man pointed down Belvedere Road to George Merrett, who was lying without moving on the pavement. He then said something strange – something that explains one of the weaknesses that ruined his life. 'I shot a man,' he said. 'You didn't think I would be a coward and *shoot a woman!*'

Henry Tarrant and the other two policemen took him to Tower Street Police Station. On the way, Tarrant said, the man was calm and obviously not drunk. It had all been a terrible accident, he said: he had shot the wrong man. At the station they found that he had a knife, as well as the gun he had killed George Merrett with.

His name was William Chester Minor. He was thirty-seven years old and the policemen had been correct; he was an army man. He was also a surgeon. He described his knife as 'a surgeon's knife. I don't always carry it with me.'

William Minor had lived in London for less than a year, at 41 Tenison Street. He was a rich man, and had no need to live in a poor area of London like Lambeth Marsh. He was also an American. He had been in the American army. This made life more complicated for the police. The American government had to be told immediately that one of their army surgeons would be on trial for murder. The 'Lambeth Marsh Tragedy' was now an international matter, important enough for the capital's police. So police from London's Scotland Yard, not from Surrey's Lambeth Marsh, now tried to find out why William Minor had killed George Merrett.

♦

William Chester Minor had come to Britain the previous autumn because he was ill. Some newspapers suggested that this illness was caused by Minor's immoral private life. By this time he had left the army because of his health. People who had met him said he was a fine, educated gentleman. But they reported that he paid for prostitutes for the night – or why would he live in an area like Lambeth Marsh? Scotland Yard had already found out that he had lived in a similar area when he had been in New York.

His room, however, showed no sign of an immoral life. It contained some excellent paintings by Minor himself, as well as a letter from John Ruskin, a well-known British painter. Mrs Fisher, who owned the house at 41 Tenison Street, said that Minor had been no trouble, but that he was a strange man. He was afraid of Irish people, and asked Mrs Fisher to tell him if any Irishmen had been seen near the house. As Lambeth Marsh had a large Irish population, this happened quite frequently.

At Minor's trial for murder that April, a policeman called Williamson told the court that Minor had gone to the police at Scotland Yard three months before the murder. He had complained that Irishmen were coming into his room and trying to poison him. Williamson had written down Minor's complaints, describing him – and this was the first use of the word to describe the unhappy American – as *insane*.

William Dennis, a man who shared a cell with Minor before the trial in April, told the court that Minor was mad. Dennis said that Minor accused him of stealing money and of trying to touch him while he slept. He looked for people under his bed.

For some months before the murder, Minor had slept with his gun under his pillow. He planned to defend himself from people who, he imagined, were going to come into his room and touch him. The people he feared were Irish.

On the night of 17 February, Minor had woken up in the middle of the night, certain that a man was standing near his bed. He reached for his gun, but the man ran away, down the stairs and out of the house. Minor followed him as fast as he could. He saw a man running down into Belvedere Road, shouted at him and then fired four times. He fired until he had hit him and the man could not hurt him.

Mrs Fisher told the court that nobody else was in the house

that night. William's brother, George Minor, told the court that when William had stayed at his home in New Haven, USA, he had had the same fears: that people wanted to get into his room and touch him. They were doing that because of something he had done while he was in the US army. He could only save himself by going to Europe. He decided to travel and paint. Then, perhaps, the people who were following him and touching him might stop making his life such hell.

The American government had found Minor a lawyer who said that the court should treat him as insane. On 6 April 1872, Minor was found legally innocent of a murder that everyone, including Minor himself, knew he had committed. He was sent to the Asylum for the Criminally Insane, Broadmoor, where Captain Surgeon William Chester Minor, previously of the United States army, became Broadmoor Patient Number 742. He had to be kept in an asylum for the criminally insane for an unlimited period of time.

Chapter 3   The Early Life of James Murray

For the last forty years of his life, James Augustus Henry Murray was the greatest and most famous editor of the *OED*. He was born in February 1827, the eldest son of a poor family in Hawick, a pretty little town near the Scottish border with England. And that was all he really wished the world to know about himself. 'I am a nobody,' he wrote towards the end of the century, '. . . ignore me completely'.

But it is impossible to ignore him because of everything he achieved as a dictionary maker. Twenty years ago his granddaughter, Elizabeth, discovered a lot of information about his childhood. It seems that although he came from a poor family, it was always clear that a great future was possible for him.

He was a serious boy, who was old for his years; he then became an amazingly clever, tall, well-built teenager with long hair and an early bright red beard that made him seem even more serious and even frightening. 'Knowledge is power,' he wrote in one of his school exercise books and added, *Nihil est melius quam vita diligentissima.** By the age of fifteen, he had some knowledge of French, Italian, German and Greek. Like all educated children then, he also knew Latin.

All kinds of knowledge were like food and drink to him. He taught himself about the flowers and rocks he saw around him; he taught himself geography and a love of maps; he found dozens of books on history and taught himself history from them; he noticed and studied everything he saw around him. His younger brothers remembered James waking them in the middle of the night to tell them that the star Sirius had appeared in the sky. It appeared exactly when and where James had calculated that it would.

He especially loved talking to very old people, who could remember events that had become part of history. He found a person who had known someone who had seen William and Mary become king and queen of England in 1689. And he loved to hear his mother tell the story of how she had heard of the victory at Waterloo in 1815.

Like most poor children at that time, he left school at fourteen. There was no money to pay for him to go to school in the town of Melrose, near his home, and anyway his parents were confident that James could teach himself. And his parents were correct. James continued to gather more and more knowledge, often because he wanted the knowledge itself, not for a particular purpose. Sometimes, though, he used the knowledge in strange ways. For example, he attempted to teach the cows in the fields near his house to come to him when he called them in Latin. He

---

* Nothing is better in life than to work hard (in Latin).

13

also read aloud the books of a Frenchman with the grand name of Théodore Agrippa d'Aubigné. He then translated them to his family, who sat round him, listening with interest and admiring the young James.

Although he could not swim, he invented a way of keeping himself on the surface of the water using plants and was rescued by friends when he nearly drowned. He taught himself to draw, and drew pictures to decorate his own writing.

By the age of seventeen, the young man who loved knowledge had become a teacher in his home town. By the age of twenty, he was in charge of a school and was helping to teach adults. At this time language had become one of his interests, both the Scottish-English that he spoke at home and older languages like Anglo-Saxon.

But all the hope of his early years was suddenly threatened, first by love and then by tragedy. In 1861, when he was only twenty-four, Murray met and then the next year married a music teacher named Maggie Scott. Their wedding picture shows that Maggie was a handsome but not very strong-looking woman. Murray at this time had long arms down to his knees, a wild beard and hair that was already thinning. His narrow eyes look neither happy nor unhappy but thoughtful.

Two years later they had a baby girl who they called Anna. But, sadly, little Anna died while still very young, as many babies did at that time. Maggie Murray then became ill herself, and the doctors did not think she could live through another long, cold Scottish winter. The doctors suggested that the Murrays should go to the south of France, where it was warm, but that was impossible on Murray's salary as a teacher.

Instead, the sad couple went to London and found a cheap place to live, in Peckham. Murray, now twenty-seven, had to stop gathering knowledge. He even had to stop his work on language, although by now he was corresponding with famous language scholars like Alexander Melville Bell, father of Alexander Graham Bell, who invented the telephone. Murray loved Maggie and he never complained, but he had to find work in a bank to earn enough money. It seemed that his story had come to a sad end.

But happily it had not. He started learning unusual languages on the way to the bank. He studied the way that Scottish policemen in London talked, to find out which part of Scotland they came from. He lectured on 'The Body'. He even noticed that as the wife he loved so much was dying, she spoke the Scottish-English of her childhood and not the London English she spoke when she taught in schools. The pleasure of this knowledge helped him a little with the pain when Maggie died.

Murray had loved and admired Maggie very much, but a year after her death he met and married Ada Ruthven. Ada's mother said she had been at school with Charlotte Brontë, and her father had a good job with the Great Indian Railways. She and Murray had a good marriage and had eleven children together, ten of them with the middle name Ruthven, as Ada's father wished.

In 1867, when he was thirty, Murray hoped to work in the British Museum. His main interest at this time was words and languages. In his letter to the museum he listed the languages he had studied: Italian, French, Catalan, Spanish and Latin were the main ones, but he had also studied Portuguese, Dutch, German and Danish. And there was also Persian, Hebrew and Aramaic Arabic, among others. Very surprisingly, Murray did not get the job at the museum, but he soon made himself feel better by studying. He studied the words used by Wowenoc Indians of Maine, USA, to count sheep. Then he compared them with the words used by the sheep farmers of Yorkshire, England, to count *their* sheep.

At this time Murray's interest in words and language was still a hobby; he did not earn his living from it. It would perhaps have stayed that way if he had not met two men. One, Alexander Ellis, taught mathematics at Trinity College, Cambridge, and the other is famous in the history of the study of language. His name was Henry Sweet. These men helped Murray to join the Philological Society.* The members of the Philological Society were some of the leading language scholars in the world. Murray had left school at fourteen and never gone to university. But when he was accepted as a member of the society, it was clear how much he had achieved as a language scholar.

Murray continued to achieve. By 1869 he was one of the people in charge of the Philological Society. In 1873 – now teaching again, at Mill Hill School, after leaving the bank – he published his first book, *The Dialects of the Southern Counties of Scotland*. The book was admired everywhere and Murray was then invited to write about the history of the English language for the *Encyclopaedia Britannica*.

As a result of this progress, Murray met other language scholars who were as great as he was. One of them was Frederick Furnivall, who was also a member of the Philological Society and one of the most amazing men in England at that time. Furnivall was a scholar of mathematics and language, but he was often criticised for being a fool. He liked women and had married and then left a servant. Both actions were considered bad behaviour in the England of Dickens's time, so many editors refused to work with him. He was, however, a brilliant scholar who, like Murray, loved to gather knowledge. Unlike Murray, he had many famous friends, like the poet Alfred Lord Tennyson; Kenneth Grahame, who wrote *The Wind in the Willows* and used Furnivall as the model for the character of Water Rat; and also John Ruskin, the painter, who also knew William Minor.

Furnivall was the second editor of the great new dictionary that

* the Philological Society: a society for the study of languages.

16

was being written at that time, and he introduced Murray to the people who were in charge of the dictionary. They were the members of Oxford University – the 'Delegates' – who published books through the publishers Oxford University Press. At that time they included some of the greatest scholars in England.

They first met Murray on 26 April 1878.

Chapter 4   The Early Life of
William Chester Minor

The beautiful, hot, tear-shaped island of Ceylon, which is now called Sri Lanka, is a place where warm winds blow from the sea and elephants walk free, and tea and coffee and strange fruits grow.

And there are the girls – young, light brown village girls who play in the sea, without clothes but unashamed, and then run along the cool, wet sand on their way back home.

William Chester Minor's clearest memories were of these girls. These young girls from Ceylon, he said later, made him want women so much that, unknowingly, they had started him on the road that ended in Broadmoor. He had first noticed their bodies when he was only thirteen years old; he was ashamed, but he could never again get the picture of women's bodies out of his mind.

Minor was born on the island in June 1834. He was born three years before James Murray and eight thousand kilometres to the east. And in one way – and one way only – the lives of the two families at different ends of the world were similar: both the Murrays and the Minors were extremely religious.

Thomas and Mary Murray were members of a religious group known as the 'Covenanters', who kept to the ways of seventeenth century Scotland. Eastman and Lucy Minor's religion was very similar, but they were missionaries. And although Eastman Strong Minor had a successful business, he finally sold it to spend all his time on his missionary work.

That was the reason that the Minor family were in Ceylon. Unlike the Murrays, the Minors were both rich and well known. Other members of the family were proud that Eastman and Lucy were spending many years away from America, bringing religious truth to people so far away from home.

Eastman and Lucy arrived in Ceylon in March 1834 and lived in a village called Manepay, on the north-east coast of the island near Trincomalee, which the British navy used as a stopping place for their ships as they sailed round the world. William was born only three months later, in June. A second child, named Lucy like her mother, was born two years later.

William played outdoors like any small boy on a warm island. He fell from a horse, he fell out of a tree. He also had some of the childhood illnesses that people in that part of the world often caught. All of this was part of a normal childhood in Ceylon.

But William Chester Minor's childhood was not at all normal. His mother died when he was three. Two years later Eastman Strong Minor went on a long journey in the east, looking for a new wife from among the people of his own religion who, like him, were missionaries from America. He left little Lucy in Ceylon, but he took William with him.

Eastman Minor met and married a woman called Judith Manchester Taylor, who came from Madison, New York. Judith Minor had the same energy as her new husband. She ran the local school, she learned the language of Ceylon, Sinhalese, and she taught it to William and later to her own children.

The school that Judith ran was excellent; it educated young William better than any school in America. He read books, he read newspapers and he learned the local languages. By the time he was twelve he spoke good Sinhalese and knew a little of other languages like Burmese, Hindi, Tamil and some Chinese. He also knew the cities of Singapore, Bangkok and Rangoon.

At the age of fourteen his parents, who had perhaps noticed how William had started to look at the girls on the beach, decided to send him back to America. They wanted him to stay with his uncle Alfred, who had a large shop in the centre of New Haven. In 1848 William left Ceylon on the first part of his journey to America – the long voyage to London.

Minor later admitted that, while he was on the ship, thoughts of women were always in his mind. He was deeply attracted to a young English girl who was there. For four weeks Minor and the girl were together as the ship went up and down on the waves. It was warm and all the women wore short dresses. Alcohol was cheap and encouraged romantic relationships.

A lot happened during those four weeks at sea, but it seems that Minor and the girl did not make love. Many years later Minor told his doctors that he had controlled his feelings, just as he had controlled his feelings about the young girls in Ceylon. His life would perhaps have been different if he had *not* controlled them.

The reason for Minor's self-control was probably guilt – a feeling that is perhaps often felt by the very religious – and not teenage shyness. From this moment, in Minor's long and unhappy life, sex and guilt became firmly tied together. Years later he apologized to his doctors on a number of occasions for his shameful thoughts about women, but he also said that he tried to fight those thoughts. He always, it seems, wanted to hide the terrible things that were in his mind from his parents – or perhaps just from the mother who died when he was three, or perhaps from his second mother.

But these feelings were still growing in the teenage Minor, and his guilt about them had not really started yet. From London he sailed to Boston and then home to his uncle in New Haven, Connecticut. He began a new life studying to be a doctor at Yale

University. His parents stayed in Ceylon for another six years and Minor spent this time working hard, keeping the pictures of women out of his mind.

He was twenty-nine in February 1863, when he finished studying at one of America's finest schools and became a doctor. He joined the army as a surgeon. The army, then called the Union Army, needed surgeons because they were fighting a war. It was a terrible war between the people of the north and the south: the American Civil War.

◆

When Minor joined the Union Army, the army of the northern states, the war was half finished, though of course the people fighting it did not know that. Eight hundred days of it had already been fought: men had seen the battles of Fort Sumter, Fort Clark, Fort Hatteras and Fort Henry, the first and second battles of Bull Run, the fights over small pieces of land at Chancellorsville, Fredericksburg, Vicksburg, Antietam, and over bridges like Mississippi's Big Black River Bridge, or islands like Island Number Ten, Missouri. The south was winning. The Union Army of the north was happy to have a surgeon from a good northern family like William Chester Minor of Yale.

Four days after Minor joined the army, on 29 June 1863, came the Battle of Gettysburg. More blood was spilled at this battle than at any other time during the war, and after it the south began to lose the war. The newspapers that Minor read each evening in New Haven reported the fighting. There were 22,000 dead on the Union side and a lot of them came from the tiny state of Connecticut, where Minor lived. During the worst of the fighting, in the first three days of July, Connecticut lost more than a quarter of the men it sent to Gettysburg. Six months later President Lincoln said that the world would never forget what the men who died in that battle had done.

There was plenty of work for a doctor in the Union Army and, as Minor's brother later told the court, William Minor could not wait to start. In 1864 he was sent south, to Virginia, to the fighting.

Then the full horror of this terrible war hit Minor, suddenly and without warning. In some ways the American Civil War was the worst war there has ever been for a soldier or for a doctor. The war was fought with new weapons which were terrible in their efficiency, machines for killing people. But it was also fought just before new medicines, like penicillin, were developed that later saved millions of lives. So the soldiers were killed and wounded with the new weapons, but they could not be helped by the new medicine.

During the battles, the doctors set up field hospitals. When a soldier was wounded they usually cut off the arm or the leg. The hospitals were dirty places where men were screaming with pain. About 360,000 Union soldiers died in the war and so did 258,000 soldiers from the south. And for every one who was killed by the new weapons, two died from the dirt and from what happened to them in the hospitals.

Minor was shocked by what he saw and heard in the hospitals. He was, as his friends at home said later, a sensitive man, too gentle to be a soldier. He read, he painted, he played music. But Virginia in 1864 was no place for a person like this. It is possible that the terrible way of life and certain events that happened at this place and at this time caused William Minor to become insane.

It is possible that the feelings that were inside him from his childhood were brought to the surface here by something that happened in Virginia early in May 1864, during another bloody battle that is known now as the Battle of the Wilderness. It was such a terrible fight that it is not surprising if sane men went mad.

◆

In the March after the Union victory at the Battle of Gettysburg, President Lincoln had put Ulysses S. Grant in charge of the Union army. Grant wanted to end the fighting over every small piece of land and every bridge and island. His plan was to kill so many soldiers in the army of the south that their army would not exist. In May 1864 the Union army moved south under Sherman to put the plan into action. It took a year, but Sherman and his army moved through Tennessee and Georgia to the final battles at Appomattox and Shreveport, which were the end of the southern army.

But at the beginning of the move south, the fighting was at its worst because the southern army was at its strongest. And because the countryside in Virginia consists of hills and woods, neither horses nor big guns could be used very much. A lot of the fighting was done by soldiers facing each other on foot. Their guns had the new and terrible bullets that could make great holes in a man. The soldiers fired the bullets into the faces and bodies of men they were close enough to touch. They started fires in the woods in which soldiers from the other side were burned to death and died in terrible pain. Doctors at the field hospitals saw men horribly injured.

And in this hell Minor first met the Irish. These were the same Irish that, Mrs Fisher of Lambeth Marsh told a London court, Minor was so frightened of. There were around 150,000 Irish soldiers in the Union army, many of them fighting together in the Irish Brigade, one of the bravest battle groups in the army.

The Irish Brigade fought at the Battle of the Wilderness and there were also Irishmen in the 28th Massachusetts, the 116th Pennsylvania and from the 63rd, 88th and 69th New York. But not all the Irish soldiers saw the war as their fight. The Irish were rivals to the American blacks for jobs that nobody else wanted to do. And the war would help the blacks, if the Union won, because Lincoln would make blacks in the south free men (which of course is what happened). Also the Irish felt that their brigade was used in all the most dangerous situations, so more Irishmen were dying than anybody else.

For both of these reasons, the Irish began to run away from the army – to desert. Not only the Irish deserted, of course; soldiers from both sides ran from the hell of these battles in large numbers. Around 287,000 soldiers from the Union side dropped their guns and ran into the forest, and 103,000 from the south. That is one in ten soldiers on the Union side and one in twelve from the south.

When a soldier was caught deserting he sometimes had his head shaved, or half shaved. Or he was forced to wear a sign with the word 'Coward' on it. Or he could be branded with the letter D for deserter on his back or on another part of his body.

The doctors branded deserters and this, it was said at the London trial, was what Minor had been forced to do. An Irishman who had deserted during the Battle of the Wilderness was brought to the sensitive young doctor from Yale to be branded. The Irishman was dirty, wild-eyed and frightened. Like many soldiers, he had started to hate the war and he wanted to go home to Ireland. He wanted to use his skill as a soldier to fight the British there.

The Irishman begged and screamed and rolled on the ground. But soldiers held him down and Minor took a hot iron letter D and pressed it, as he had been told, on the Irishman's cheek. Minor could smell the Irishman's face burn. Then the man was taken away, screaming and holding his face.

After the pain in his face had ended, the Irishman had no future. In America his face would tell everyone that he was a coward. In England or Ireland every policeman could see that he had fought in America and deserted. He could not now fight against the British on the streets of Ireland; he was too obviously a criminal. And who could he hate for what happened to him?

- Brand: N. Mark / stamp
  V. Mark

The doctor who had not helped the injured, as a doctor should, but who had branded him on the face. At least, that is what Minor thought was in the man's mind. He feared that other Irishmen would take revenge for what had happened to a member of the Irish Brigade, and so eventually he was afraid of all Irishmen.

Minor himself, in 1915, when he was an old man, told quite a different story. But until that time people thought that this was what had driven Minor mad. 'He branded an Irishman during the American Civil War,' they used to say. 'It drove him mad.'

◆

A week or so later, Minor, who appeared unchanged by the branding experience, was sent to safer hospitals in the north. He worked at several, but then a letter came from the hospital where he had worked in New Haven. It asked for his return, as his work had been so good. This was unusual, but some of the 5,500 assistant surgeons (as Minor was) were not really doctors at all.

By the autumn of 1866 Minor had risen to be a captain, working as a surgeon in a hospital in New York. Before he became a captain, Minor seemed healthy in body and mind. But during his time in New York he began to carry a gun when he was not wearing his uniform, which was illegal. Minor himself explained this by saying that a friend, another captain in the army, had been attacked and robbed while he was returning from a bar in New York. Minor feared that he would be attacked too. This was perhaps the start of insane fears that ended in the murder at Lambeth Marsh.

Minor started to visit wild bars and spend every night with prostitutes. He returned to the hospital early in the morning, tired after spending his nights in this way. The other doctors were worried about Minor. The sensitive doctor was behaving strangely. Also, the prostitutes were giving him diseases.

In 1867 his father, Eastman, died in New Haven. Minor surprised the other doctors. He told them he was going to marry a young woman who lived in the Manhattan area of New York. Nobody has ever discovered who this woman was, but some of the doctors at Minor's hospital thought it was a dancer or a prostitute. It seems that Minor met the woman's mother, who thought that there was something strange about the young captain. She stopped the wedding. In later years Minor always refused to discuss what had happened, or to give the woman's name. But the other doctors at the hospital thought he was angry about it at the time.

The army was unhappy about the change in Captain Minor and the way he was spending his time. They sent him to the country, to Fort Barrancas, Florida. Although Minor was still a captain, he was given a much less important job than he had had before.

Minor was angry with the army. He missed the prostitutes he visited in New York. Sometimes he was very angry with his colleagues; at other times he painted and became quieter. He thought that the other doctors were talking about him, and he fought one of them. Minor seemed strange and a little mad.

During the summer of 1868, he said he had stayed too long in the Florida sun. He began to get terrible headaches. He was sent back to his old hospital in New York as a patient. By September it was clear that he was very ill. For the first time, the idea that he was insane appeared in a report.

The report was signed by Surgeon Hammond on 3 September 1868. Minor could not, said the report, get one idea out of his head, and it had taken over his mind. The report did not say what that one idea was. But his mind was not now in the real world. Minor was just thirty-four years old: his life and his mind were out of his control. He was sent to the Government Hospital for the Insane in Washington DC.

Minor stayed there for eighteen months. He was allowed to walk outside in the gardens and also go into Washington. The army was still paying his captain's salary. But the doctors at the hospital were not hopeful that Minor would ever recover. The following April, Minor had to retire from the army, but the army continued to pay him for the rest of his life.

♦

In February 1871 Minor left the asylum to stay with a doctor friend on West 20th Street in Manhattan, New York. A few weeks later he went home to spend the summer with his brother Alfred. He saw his old friends at Yale and worked at the Minor family shop, which Alfred and his older brother George ran at 261 Chapel Street. The summer and autumn of 1871 were the last free and happy American days that Minor ever enjoyed.

In October, Minor went by ship from Boston to London. He planned to spend a year or two in Europe, he told his friends. He would rest, read, paint. He would visit Paris, Rome and Venice. He would rest his mind. He would contact painters in London. He would recover. He would return to America a new man.

In November he arrived in London and took a room at a hotel. He had money with him, his books and his paints.

He also had his gun.

Chapter 5   Dictionaries Before the *OED*

The English dictionary – a list of all the most useful English words, arranged in alphabetical order with explanations of their meanings – is quite a new idea. Four hundred years ago there were no monolingual dictionaries, as we know them, with words listed in alphabetical order.

There were no dictionaries, for example, when William

Shakespeare was writing his plays. Shakespeare used a lot of new words, and he used existing words in new ways, but he could not check either the spelling or the meaning of those words. That is not only because there were no dictionaries; it was because Shakespeare could not, as we say today, *look something up.*

That is because the phrase *look something up,* meaning *look for something in a dictionary,* did not exist. It did not appear in the English language until 1692, when it was used by an Oxford history scholar named Anthony Wood.

As the phrase did not exist until the early seventeenth century, the idea did not exist either. So when Shakespeare, in his play *Twelfth Night,* wrote about a hotel called *The Elephant,* he did not perhaps know what an elephant was – he certainly had not seen one (unlike William Chester Minor). He also did not know why hotels were given this name. He had no way of checking if the hotel in his play really would be named *The Elephant.* One or two hotels in London had that name, but Shakespeare's play took place in Illyria.

In Shakespeare's time there were plenty of books of maps, there were books of prayers, books about science, books about people's lives and books of love stories. But no dictionaries. When Shakespeare wrote about Greece and Rome, he used a book by Thomas Cooper which listed information about those places and the people in them. We know this because some of Cooper's information is wrong and the wrong information is in the plays. But that was almost all the help he had.

The need for a dictionary with all the words listed in alphabetical order was felt in Shakespeare's time. Just before Shakespeare's death, his friend John Webster wrote in his play *The Duchess of Malfi,* 'What's that (word)? I need a dictionary . . .'

Although there were no dictionaries, as we know them, available to Shakespeare, some books called dictionaries had been published. There was a book of Latin words published as a

Dictionarius in 1225. In 1538 the first of a series of Latin–English dictionaries appeared in London: Thomas Elyot's word-list, which was the first book to use the English word *dictionary* in its title. Almost twenty years later a man named John Withals published a dictionary for young people in Latin and English, but the words were not listed in alphabetical order. They were listed by subject – for example, *the names of birds* or *water birds*.

In 1604 a teacher named Robert Cawdrey used other books to produce an alphabetical list of words. It was a small book of 120 pages, about 2,500 word entries. It had only 'hard, unusual English words', as the title said, but it was still the first monolingual English dictionary.

For the next century and a half, dictionary after dictionary was published. Each one was larger than the last, and each said it was better at educating the people who needed educating. For all of the seventeenth century these books listed, as Cawdrey's had, only 'hard words' – words that were unusual in one way or another. The editors of these dictionaries thought that the small number of entries was an advantage to the dictionary user. They were proud of the choice of words they had included. In fact some words were created so that they could be included in dictionaries!

The definitions in these early dictionaries were not as long as the definitions in dictionaries today. They were often only one word, although in some dictionaries the definitions were very long.

Seven dictionaries were written and published in seventeenth century England, the last one with 38,000 entries. But still there was no dictionary that tried to list *all* the words of the language – the easy words as well as the difficult ones. And still the dictionary makers were not using all the words that were spoken and written before they started writing the dictionary.

By the seventeenth century English was beginning to be the

world language that it is today. But there was no record of all the words in the language, and no alphabetical list of them in dictionaries. The situation in other countries – Italy, France, Germany – was different.

The Accademia della Crusca in Florence had been responsible for Italian culture and the Italian language since 1582, three hundred years before there was a country by the name of 'Italy'. The Accademia produced a dictionary of the Italian language in 1612.

In France the Académie Française has told the French people what can be and what cannot be accepted as 'good French' since it began in 1634.

By the eighteenth century the British had begun to realize that they, too, needed to know more about their language, to study it more, and to make it more important than other languages.

As a result, dictionaries improved greatly during the first half of the eighteenth century. The first dictionary that included easy words as well as hard words appeared, edited by Nathaniel Bailey. Very little is known about Bailey; he owned a school, he was a member of a religious group called the Seventh-day Baptist Church – that is all we know. But he produced twenty-five editions of his dictionary between 1721 and 1782. All the editions sold well.

The front page of the first edition gives an idea of the enormous amount of work that is needed to produce a dictionary of all the words in the English language. On the front page Bailey tells us that his dictionary explains which language each word has come from. Some words in English have come from Old English, others from French, Spanish, Italian, Dutch and many other languages. The Bailey dictionary also gives definitions of difficult words, explains words used in subjects like medicine and lists names of people and places in Britain. It also tries to explain well-known phrases. But it was still not a complete record of all the words in the English language, listed alphabetically.

The next man who tried was one of the most famous people in the history of English language and literature. And even two centuries after he wrote his dictionary, in the opinion of everyone who has read it, Samuel Johnson's *A Dictionary of the English Language* is, and always will be, a great dictionary.

You can still find this wonderful book, with its beautiful leather cover and thick paper, today. It is almost too heavy to carry and needs to be read on a desk. It gives readers a lot of pleasure, as they read or look up words. For example, the word that Shakespeare was unable to look up: *elephant*. Johnson gives the reader a long paragraph of information about the elephant. He tells the reader what sort of animal the elephant is, what it eats, how it has sex and how to catch one.

The entry, like all the entries, is full of interest, detail and charm. But Johnson's dictionary was also very important in the history of the English language; only the *OED* was more important.

◆

Samuel Johnson had been thinking about and planning his dictionary for many years before he started writing. Johnson was a teacher who had become a writer for a magazine called the *Gentleman's Magazine* and he wanted to be more well known than he was.

But he also wanted to satisfy the need for a complete dictionary. By the middle of the eighteenth century, when people said 'a complete dictionary' they meant a record of the language and an alphabetical list of all the words. But they also thought a dictionary should fix the limits of each word. The idea of *fixing* has been important in dictionary-making since this time. Without it, it was felt, we have no control over how the words in the language are used.

The people calling for the *fixing*, the controlling of the limits of words, were some of the great writers of the eighteenth century. They included Addison, Pope, Defoe, Dryden and Swift. Some, like Swift, wanted spelling and even pronunciation fixed, as well as meaning. Many wanted something like the French Académie Française to be started in England to do the fixing.

The same need for limits was felt in science, especially physics. The limits of colours were also being fixed. Questions were asked like, 'What is blue?' 'What is yellow?' And in other areas of physics, 'How hot is boiling water?'

The need to be certain was also expressed in the search for an instrument that would tell ships exactly where they were at sea. The dictionary was compared to this instrument. It would show the way through the sea of words. The instrument would stop the ship crashing on the rocks by fixing its position, east and west and (more difficult) north and south. The dictionary would fix the meaning of words. It would stop people using words wrongly and so stop words losing their meaning.

Scholars now disagree about whether Johnson aimed to fix the meanings of words when he started his dictionary. Most scholars now think that Johnson started with this aim. But after about three years he realized that the aim was impossible, and also that fixing meanings was not such a good idea.

Another dictionary writer, Benjamin Martin, argued against the attempt to use dictionaries to fix meanings. He wrote that language will always change; it is in the nature of language to change. So any attempt to fix the meanings of words will always fail.

But it was not the need for a dictionary, nor the discussion about fixing meaning, that started Samuel Johnson writing his dictionary. It was money. In 1746 a group of five London booksellers (the famous Thomas Longman was one of them) knew that a new dictionary would sell well. They knew that

Samuel Johnson wanted to write one and they knew he did not have much money. They offered him money to start writing the dictionary and more when he had finished.

Samuel Johnson was thirty-seven years old in 1746. He used part of the money the booksellers gave him to take rooms in Fleet Street. He also paid six men (five of them from Scotland, like James Murray) to help him. Like Murray a century later, Johnson decided that the only way to write a complete dictionary was to read the whole of literature and list every word.

There are two other ways of listing words for a dictionary. You can list words that people say and you can use words from other dictionaries. Johnson thought the first way was too difficult. The second way was possible, but it was not as important as the third way, which was reading.

Even with six helpers, Johnson quickly realized that there had to be limits. It was impossible to read everything in literature. He decided to read nothing earlier than Shakespeare's time, except Chaucer.

So Johnson and his helpers bought or borrowed books, read them, marked the words he wanted for the dictionary, and wrote the sentences with the words in them on slips of paper. And these quoted meanings are the great strength of Johnson's dictionary. For example, there are 134 entries for the word *take*, all with quotations showing the meaning.

Johnson and his helpers finished listing words in 1750. He spent the next four years choosing the 118,000 quotations (and changing some that he didn't like). Finally, he finished the definitions of all the entries. Some of these definitions he wrote himself and some were borrowed from other writers. (The *elephant* definition was partly borrowed.)

The dictionary was finally published by Longman in 1755. There were four editions in Johnson's lifetime. It sold very well and was praised by almost everybody, although there was some criticism. Some people thought that Johnson's use of his own ideas (and jokes) in the definitions meant that the book could not be used to fix meanings. There was also criticism of the choice of quotations. And some of the definitions were too simple and some too complicated, according to other criticisms.

But there was praise from the great French writer, Voltaire. There was praise from Accademia della Crusca, in Florence. And over a century later, James Murray said that when people referred to 'the Dictionary', they meant Samuel Johnson's dictionary.

Chapter 6   The Start of the *OED*

The date was 5 November 1857. The time was just after six. The place was a house at the north-west corner of St James's Square, in a rich and fashionable area in the centre of London. It was near the best shops and the prettiest churches.

The house was a private library; the London Library, whose books are available to anyone who pays to join. In 1857 the library had a few thousand books in it, and there was space for more. Some rooms in the house were empty, so the London Library made them available for talks and meetings, especially to groups of scholars. The Philological Society met there every two weeks.

On this cold Thursday evening, the speaker was Richard Chenevix Trench. Like many of the other 200 members of the Philological Society, Chenevix Trench believed in spreading the English language round the world as enthusiastically as other people believed in their religion. Chenevix Trench had a high position in the Church of England. For him the growth of English was a way of helping Englishmen to spread religion, especially the Church of England's view of religion.

Sixty members of the Philological Society were there for this meeting. They were scholars and they knew a lot about language – other languages and their own. They had come to listen to Chenevix Trench talk about dictionaries.

Chenevix Trench stood in front of his audience. He stood with difficulty because many years ago he had broken both knees in a fall. He spoke about the weak points of dictionaries that were available at that time.

But then he said something more important for the future of dictionary-making. He said that a dictionary should be a list of the language. It was not a guide to the correct use of words. Words should not be chosen for the dictionary because they were 'good' or not chosen because they were 'bad'. The dictionary-maker's job was not criticism. He was a recorder of words and meanings as they were at a particular time. So neither Samuel Johnson in England nor the Académie Française in France should tell anybody which words to use. A dictionary should record *all* words.

A dictionary should also contain, Chenevix Trench told his listeners, the history of every word, even of words that were not used now. It should be possible to look in a dictionary and see when a word was first used, all its various uses in its lifetime and then (sometimes) its last use with the date of that last use. A dictionary, in other words, should show the life story of every word in it. Each part of the life story of each word should be shown, said Chenevix Trench, by quotations. Chenevix Trench meant the life story of every word as it was *written*; the life story of every word as it was spoken would be impossible.

Johnson's dictionary had included quotations, of course, but his quotations had shown only *meaning* (or the meaning at the time). Chenevix Trench wanted quotations that would show the history of meaning: a different quotation for every meaning the word had ever had as it changed with use. That meant that every book that had ever used each word would be read. Every different meaning through history would be written down in a quotation. The amount of work would be enormous, and most people at this time thought it would be impossible.

But Chenevix Trench had an idea that made it possible. Clearly one person could not do all the necessary reading and nor could a team of people, as Samuel Johnson had used. There would have to be contributions from hundreds and hundreds of people, all reading books unpaid and in their own free time.

The idea does not seem new or unusual today but nobody had suggested it before. The members of the Philological Society liked the idea. A dictionary recorded by hundreds of people seemed to suit the idea of a dictionary that did not tell people how they should use words. Both ideas put the people above the dictionary, not below it.

There was already a group of people from the Philological Society, a group which included Chenevix Trench and Furnivall, who were listing words that were not listed in the dictionaries of the day. They intended to publish this list as a supplement to published dictionaries. But it quickly became clear that this supplement would be bigger than any published dictionary, including Johnson's. So on 7 January 1858 the idea of a completely new dictionary was accepted by the Philological Society. This date is usually accepted as the start of the *Oxford English Dictionary*.

Frederick Furnivall then asked for readers to read books in their own time and unpaid. They could choose which time in history they wanted to read books from: 1250–1526, 1526–1674 or 1674 to the present (1858).

The readers were asked to read and make word-lists from everything they read. Also, the Society asked them to look for certain words. Each reader should take a slip of paper and write the word at the top, on the left. Below that, also on the left, they should write the details of the book they were reading: these were, in order, the date, author, title of the book and page number. Below that the reader should write the full sentence quotation that contained the word. Exactly the same way of making dictionaries is still used today.

The dictionary's first name was the *New English Dictionary on Historical Principles* and the first editor was Herbert Coleridge (son of the poet Samuel Taylor Coleridge). Coleridge designed a desk to contain the 60,000 to 100,000 slips of paper that the readers were going to send him. He thought that the first book of the dictionary would be ready within two years. And if the readers were not so slow, said a clearly unhappy Coleridge, the book would be ready even more quickly.

All of this was very wrong. More than six *million* slips of paper came in from the readers and it took twenty years, not two, before the first book of the dictionary was ready. At the beginning nobody understood how much work the dictionary would need.

Coleridge died after only two years at work, at the age of thirty-one. He was not even half-way through looking at the quotations of words beginning with *A*. He had been caught in the rain on the way to a Philological Society lecture and kept his wet coat on in the cold room. He was ill the next day and died a short time later.

Frederick Furnivall was the new editor. He worked with his usual energy, but he was a man who always made enemies. One of his good ideas was to use a team of assistants, so that the editor did not have to read every slip of paper from the readers himself. The assistants checked and grouped the slips of paper before the editor saw them.

The editor chose a word to work on. Then the search for the earliest quotation started, then the quotations were put in date order, showing how the word changed over the centuries, until the present time.

But for reasons nobody really understands, the dictionary started to die while Furnivall was editor. The readers stopped reading and stopped sending in their slips of paper. Many readers returned books that Furnivall had sent them before they had even started the work. Furnivall spent less and less time working on the dictionary, and more and more time with women. By 1868 it seemed that work on the dictionary would stop completely.

But Furnivall did not let the dictionary die. By this time Murray was a leading member of the Philological Society. He was just over forty and teaching at Mill Hill School. Furnivall asked him to become editor and he asked Oxford University Press to publish the dictionary.

Murray was persuaded to produce some pages showing how four different words would appear in the dictionary. These pages were shown to the Delegates of Oxford University Press. Furnivall was also talking to other publishers, but he quickly had an argument with one of them – Macmillan.

Then came bad news. Oxford University Press did not like Murray's pages. They asked how hard Murray had looked for quotations. They did not like the work on pronunciation, and they discussed removing Murray's work on the languages that the four words had originally come from. Cambridge University Press, when asked by Murray and Furnivall, were not interested at all. So discussions continued with Oxford, and slowly they accepted Murray's pages and they accepted him as editor.

On 26 April 1878 Murray met the Delegates for the first time. He expected to be frightened of the great scholars, all much older than he was, but to his surprise he liked them and they liked him. The Delegates decided that OUP would publish the dictionary and Murray would be the new editor.

Another year was spent talking about money, though Murray often left the details to his wife, Ada. So work actually started on

1 March 1879, nearly twenty years after Chenevix Trench's lecture at the Philological Society. The dictionary would be 7,000 pages long and it would take ten years to write. In fact it took a lot longer than this. But work now started again, and this time it never stopped.

Murray had a work-room built in the gardens at Mill Hill School, where he could edit the dictionary. Then he wrote a four-page letter asking for new readers to find words and quotations. The four-page letter went to magazines and newspapers as well as bookshops and libraries. Sometimes the letter was put inside books in libraries.

This was how, at some time in the early 1880s, the letter was seen by William Minor. He opened a book in his cell on the top floor of Block 2 of the Broadmoor Asylum for the Criminally Insane in Crowthorne, Berkshire, and one of Murray's letters fell out. By this time books had become a second life for William Minor – one of his two cells had books in it from floor to ceiling. He was very interested in Murray's letter.

Chapter 7   The Early Years in Broadmoor

'Minor. William Chester. A thin man with light-coloured hair and high cheeks. He is thirty-eight years old, is well educated, but has no known religion. He has been sent to Broadmoor as "dangerous to others". He went to trial for the murder of George Merrett of Lambeth but was found not guilty because of insanity. He says that other people have been trying to poison him for years.'

That is the first paragraph of the notes made about Broadmoor Patient Number 742, William Chester Minor, on the afternoon of the day he was brought to Broadmoor – Wednesday 17 April 1872. Guards had brought Minor, in chains, by train and coach from prison in Newington in Surrey. He was brought to the front gate. Behind them were two thick green wooden doors and then more heavy gates.

Inside Broadmoor, Minor was told to get out of the coach. He was searched and then his chains were taken off and were taken back to the prison in Surrey. The person in charge of the asylum at that time was a kind man named William Orange. His assistant signed the receipt which said that Minor had arrived.

Minor was taken to Block 4, where new arrivals were interviewed and notes made. He heard the horses turn round, heard the guards get back in the coach and order the driver to return to the railway station. He heard the gates open to let the coach out and then close again. One set of gates was chained closed. He was now inside Broadmoor, locked into a place which could be his home for the rest of his life.

It was a fairly new home. Broadmoor had been open just nine years. The old asylum at Lambeth, less than two kilometres from the place where William Minor had murdered George Merrett, was full. The courts had been sending people who were guilty but insane to asylums since 1800, and most were now full.

All the asylums at that time looked like prisons. Broadmoor had been designed by a man who designed prisons. There were long cell blocks, high walls with broken glass on top of them, and the windows had bars. As asylums were prisons, not hospitals, the people in them were criminals, not hospital patients, although they were not badly treated.

But Minor, an American murderer – where should they put him? There were six blocks for men and two for women. If it was thought that a patient might try to kill himself, he was put in a cell in Block 6 and watched all the time. People who were ill or might hurt themselves were put in Block 1, which had special cells with thick, soft material on the inside walls. If someone was dangerous, he also went to Block 6 because there were more staff on that block.

The first few days at Broadmoor were always spent asking the patient about himself and about the crime. After that the patient was never asked about the crime again. The Broadmoor doctors decided to send Minor – who, of course, was a doctor himself – to Block 2. This was the most comfortable of all the six blocks; it was often used for patients who would be sent home soon. It had even been compared once, by a visitor, to one of the famous London gentleman's clubs.

But Minor was especially well treated. All the staff knew that he was a well-educated man who had been in the American army, and that the American government still paid him. So he was given not one cell but two, a pair of connected rooms that were only locked at night. But he was watched through bars in the door.

The windows, too, had iron bars, but there was a lovely view through them. Minor could see the Broadmoor tennis courts, cows in the fields and tree-covered hills in the distance. In the spring he could hear the birds from his cell.

The guard sat outside the cells, watching twenty men on his floor. He let them in and out of their rooms to visit the bathroom. He had a gas flame burning beside him so the patients could light their cigarettes; they were not allowed to have matches, but tobacco was provided.

The American government did not forget Minor either. A letter came to Broadmoor. Would it be possible for 'our poor friend' to have in his cell some of the things he had with him in his room at Lambeth Marsh? And could food and coffee be sent to Dr Minor? Mr Orange replied that Dr Minor could have whatever he liked, if it was not dangerous in any way.

A week later clothes arrived for Dr Minor, with his photographs, pipes, and also a map of London and a watch. The watch had been mentioned at the trial. It had been owned by the Minor family for a long time.

But most important to him, Dr Orange said later, were the paints and pencils and drawing paper. He could now do something useful in his cell, which all patients were encouraged to do.

Over the next few months Minor made his cell a comfortable place. It did look a little like a gentleman's club. He had money: about twelve hundred dollars a year. It was paid to his brother Alfred in Connecticut, because Minor was not well enough to be given money. Alfred sent the money to England as soon as he received it, and Minor used it for books.

First he asked for his own books to be sent from New Haven. When they were in his cell, he ordered hundreds of new and second-hand books from the London booksellers. At first, the books stood in piles in his cell. Later he asked and paid for bookshelves to be built. In the end, one of his two rooms became a library, with a writing desk, a couple of chairs and bookshelves from floor to ceiling. His paint, pencils and drawing paper were in the other room. He also had a few bottles of wine.

Minor was also a musician. He played several musical instruments and taught other patients to play them. He was allowed, and could afford, to pay other patients to clean his cell. It was a comfortable life in the two rooms in Block 2. He was warm and he ate fairly well. There were doctors if he was ill. He could walk in the Broadmoor gardens. He could paint and read as much as he wanted to.

But there was no doubt that he was still insane. The terrible ideas and pictures in his mind grew stronger as the years passed, although he was never ill enough to go to Block 6 or Block 1.

These terrible things in his mind always happened to him at night. Small boys climbed into his room, he believed, gave him something to make him sleep and then had sex with him. It was never quite clear, though, whether he thought he was having sex with the boys or with the women he dreamed of all the time.

April 1873: 'Dr Minor is thin and pale. He seems sane during the day and he paints and plays his musical instruments. But at night he puts his furniture against the door to stop anyone coming in.'

June 1875: 'The doctor thinks that people are coming into his cell from under the floor or through the windows. He thinks they put poison in his mouth. He wants to be weighed every month in case the poison is making him heavier.'

August 1875: 'He often looks wild and frightened in the morning, as if he hasn't had much sleep. He says he feels as if a cold iron is being pressed against his teeth at night and that something is being put into his body.'

A year later another patient said that Minor had come to see him in his cell. Minor had said he would give the other patient everything if he would cut his – Dr Minor's – throat. A guard was ordered to look after Dr Minor.

Another year later he said that his night-visitors were cutting open his heart and taking the liquids from his body. They were coming into his cell through the floor. In 1878 he said that electricity was being passed through his body. Electric buttons were placed on his forehead. He was put in a coach and taken across the countryside. He was taken as far as Constantinople, he told a guard once, where he had to have sex in public.

All these terrible imaginary events were getting stronger in Minor's mind, but at the same time a more scholarly and thoughtful side was growing in Minor too. 'When he is not talking about his night-visitors,' said one report, 'he talks very intelligently about most subjects. He works in his bit of garden and is fairly cheerful just now – but he has days when he goes quieter.' A year later the same doctor wrote: 'His mind is clear and he speaks intelligently most of the time.'

He also began to think of Broadmoor as his home and the guards as his family. 'He does not want to go back to America now, as he did before,' one doctor wrote. 'He would like a little bit more freedom, to see London perhaps, or perhaps to visit a flower show.' But the same doctor had no doubt that, 'Dr Minor is . . . more insane than he was some years ago. He thinks that he is visited almost nightly.'

At about this time Minor became truly sorry for what he had done. He knew already that the American government had sent money to Eliza Merrett, George's widow, and so had Judith Minor, but now he wrote to her.

He explained that he was very sorry for what he had done. He offered to help her in any way he could, perhaps by arranging to send money to her children. Eliza accepted money from Minor and also asked if it might be possible to visit him.

It was very unusual for the widow of a murdered man to visit the man who had killed him, but Dr Orange allowed it. So some time during late 1879, Eliza travelled from Lambeth to Broadmoor. There she met the man who had ended her husband's life seven years before, and changed her own life and the lives of her seven children.

According to William Orange's notes, the meeting was difficult at first but it progressed well, and before the end of the visit Eliza had agreed to come again. Soon she was visiting every month. She was never really a friend, but she clearly was not afraid of Minor either. She knew very little about books – she could hardly read – but she agreed to bring him books from booksellers in London, so he would get his books more quickly than through the post.

Eliza probably brought books for a few months only. She started to drink too much and eventually lost interest in Minor. But in early 1880 he opened one of the books Eliza had brought and found one of the 2,000 letters that Murray had had printed in April 1879, asking for readers.

Minor read in Murray's letter that 'in the Early English period before the invention of printing . . . little outside help is needed.'

But from 'the later sixteenth century . . . several books remain to be read.' There was work to be done in seventeenth century literature and even some in the nineteenth century, especially the very recent books. 'But it is in the eighteenth century above all that help is urgently needed.' Especially, it seemed 'the eighteenth century literature . . . of the United States'. American scholars had not done the reading, and so now Murray was looking for English readers.

Murray also listed more than 200 authors whose work needed to be read for the dictionary. Some of the books were unusual, though Murray could send some of them from Mill Hill – if people promised to send them back. Under Furnivall, some of the readers treated the dictionary like a library, but kept the books.

Minor wrote to Murray, offering to be a reader. We do not know exactly when this was. Murray later said that he had received Minor's letter very soon after he had started the dictionary. It is possible that Minor started work as a reader in either 1880 or 1881. By this time Murray had already received about 800 replies to his letter, so he had no time to wonder about the address at the top of Minor's letter.

Murray replied, politely as usual, saying that Minor should start reading immediately. He could either start with his own books or come to Mill Hill to borrow some. Later, there might be requests for a certain word, but not yet.

Chapter 8   Dr Minor's Work on the *OED*

Murray wrote to Minor, instructing him on the work of a contributor. If Eliza Merrett's visits to Minor were a sign to him that the world had forgiven him for his crime, then perhaps Minor understood Murray's letter in the same way. The letter made him a member of society again, someone who lived in a corner of the real world, even if his corner was two cells in an asylum in a foreign country. It connected him, again, to the world of learning and comfort outside his cell.

Minor was by now almost fifty but looked like an old man. After ten years with nobody of his own intelligence to talk to, he felt that he was once again among scholars like himself. And he began to regain, in a small way, a sense of his own value. From his doctor's reports, it seems that Minor was more confident and more content as soon as he began his work on the dictionary. He became, if only for a short time, a new man.

But the work that had made such a difference to Minor also created new problems for him. Minor saw immediately how important the dictionary was; important to history, to the future and to the English-speaking world. It was also an enormous amount of work. Murray's letter had explained that the dictionary would need *hundreds of thousands of quotations*. Could all this be done from an asylum cell?

William Minor was insane, but he knew very well where he was and why he was there. Could he be a part of this great work?

He found his answers to these questions in his belief first that the new dictionary was necessary, and second that Murray was working on it in the correct way. Minor worked on the dictionary because it gave him something interesting to do, but also because he believed in it.

And suddenly his books, which had been just a way of taking his mind out of his cell, became the most important part of his life. For a time he could forget what the night-visitors were trying to do to him; he needed only to keep his books safe. For the next twenty years he did almost nothing at Broadmoor except live in the world of books and, as he read their words, try to forget his damaged mind.

Fortunately Murray's plan meant that Minor would have to go much deeper into the words than just reading them. He now needed to read widely and with care, so that the best possible entries were chosen for the dictionary.

But, Minor and many other contributors wanted to know, which words were possible entries in the dictionary and which words were not?

Murray's rules about this were clear: *every* word was a possible dictionary entry. Readers should try to find a quotation for each and every word in a book. They should perhaps look especially hard for words that they thought were difficult or unusual or used in a new way. But they should look for ordinary words as well, if a sentence said something about the use or meaning of the word. Special attention needed to be paid to the first date that a word was used, so that the word's introduction into the language could be fixed.

The date of each quotation was so important that it was written just below the entry itself at the top left corner of each slip of paper that the contributor used. Some of these slips of paper were printed and sent out from Murray's office at Mill Hill, but for the less well-known books Murray asked contributors to write out their own slips of paper.

Another question that William Minor and many other contributors asked was how many quotations should be sent to Mill Hill for each word? As many quotations as convenient, replied Murray, especially if each quotation helped to explain a different meaning. The floors of the Mill Hill office had been made stronger so they could hold all that paper.

Murray did not tell Minor or any other contributor what had happened to some of the slips of paper when Furnivall was editor. Some had been eaten by rats. Some had got wet and were now unreadable. Some were unreadable although they had not got wet, because the contributors' writing was so difficult to read. Murray wrote to a friend that some would be easier to read if they were written in Chinese. Some, beginning with the letter *I*, had been left in a box at someone's house, and all of the letter *F* had been sent to Florence by accident.

Murray sent detailed instructions about posting slips to Mill Hill – money was available to pay the cost of posting. He also sent many patient letters to contributors who still did not understand what to do. (Minor was not one of them.) For example, one contributor complained that she had read a 750 page book and could not find any entries for the dictionary. Many early contributors asked if every sentence with a word like *the* should be a different entry with its own slip of paper. It is clear from the letters of these confused contributors why a scholar like William Chester Minor was so helpful to the dictionary.

Minor read the instructions carefully and understood them. He looked at the shelves of books he had collected over ten years in his library-cell. He took out the list of books that had come with Murray's original letter.

Minor had plenty of time and he certainly had plenty of books. He was the sort of man who never did exactly what he was told. So, although he believed in Murray's method, he spent his first few weeks as a contributor thinking of a different and even better way of working.

He took down from his shelves the first of his books, put it on the desk in his cell and opened it. Perhaps it was a French book called *Compleat Woman* by Jacques Du Bosc, published in London in 1693. It had been translated by a man whose name was given only as 'NN'.

There were many reasons for starting with this book. It was a good seventeenth century book. It was unusual and probably full of unusual words. And Murray had asked for entries from books of this time.

So Minor took from a drawer a large piece of white paper, a bottle of black ink and one of his best pens. Then he folded the paper in half three times, so that he had eight small sides of paper to write on. Then, with perhaps one last look out of the window at the lovely view from his cell, he began to read the book, slowly, paragraph by paragraph. As he read, he began the routine he had planned over the last few weeks, before he started work.

It was a way of working that was admired by Murray and his assistants at Mill Hill at the time and, as his eight-sided pieces of paper have been kept, it is still admired today.

Each time Minor found a word that he thought was interesting, he wrote it and the quotation in tiny letters in the correct place on one of the eight sides of paper. He left space above and below it for other words beginning with the same letter. In this way he was creating his own alphabetical list as he read. But he worked so carefully that he nearly always left exactly the right amount of space above and below the first words he found.

Sometimes the same word was found more than once. For example, the word *feel* was noted on sixteen of Du Bosc's pages, including the word *feeling*.

It probably took Minor many weeks, perhaps months, to complete this first word-list. Perhaps it was late in the year 1883 by the time he had finished it. It was now at least two years, and perhaps more, since he had started work as a reader, but still he had not sent one slip of paper back to Mill Hill. Perhaps Murray and his assistants thought he had lost interest in the dictionary.

But the opposite was true. As soon as Minor had finished his word-list from the first book, he started work on another book. Perhaps his next book was Francis Junius's *The Painting of the Ancients*, 1638, or Thomas Wilson's *The Rule of Reason*, 1551. Perhaps it was something quite different. We cannot be sure which of his books he read first, although we know some of the titles of the books he made word-lists from. Most of them show his interest in history and (perhaps sadly) travel. At least one book that he read and made a word-list from was about Ceylon, where he had lived as a boy.

It took him about three months to complete one of his word-lists for each book. He worked hard all day, while the guards checked him every hour. The pieces of folded paper piled up on his desk. By the autumn of 1884 he had so many of them that he asked Murray which words were especially needed, because he felt sure he could send them in from the lists on his desk.

From that year Minor worked in a different way from other contributors. They chose a book and sent slips to Mill Hill, and later to Oxford, when Murray and his editors moved there. Minor, on the other hand, asked Murray which words he needed for the dictionary and sent them in from his own word-lists. He had even made a key to his own word-list, a dictionary within a dictionary, which meant that he could find any word that Murray wanted, immediately.

This, of course, made life much easier for Murray and his hard-working assistants. When a word was needed for the dictionary, they did not have to search through hundreds or even thousands of slips of paper; they could just write to Crowthorne and ask for it.

Usually they very quickly received a letter and the quotation slips from Minor, with information that was so complete and so accurate that it could go straight into the dictionary.

For example, the entry for the word *dirt* in the *OED* was written by Minor. He was usually able to find the first use of any word he worked on – something which was very important to the *OED* then and now. For the use of the word *dirt* meaning 'earth' he quotes from John Fryer's *New Account of East India and Persia,* published in 1698.

Sometimes Minor worked almost too hard. Murray wrote to another editor that he wished he had 'about half the number' of quotations from Minor, but he added that they might be useful later.

Strangely, the enormous amount of work that Minor did for the dictionary was a little less at one time of the year: in summer fewer slips arrived from Crowthorne. The editors thought that perhaps Dr Minor enjoyed the warm days outside, away from his books. But when autumn started again, and the evenings were darker, every word that Murray needed an entry for was provided from Crowthorne, with more quotations than the editors could use.

Minor sent a total of 10,000 slips to Murray. But this number does not explain his importance to the dictionary – other contributors sent in more. Almost all of Minor's slips were used in the dictionary, and nearly all of them had been requested by the editors. His slips, in other words, were more useful to the dictionary than those sent in by other contributors.

The editors were grateful to Minor. The first book of the dictionary, *A–B*, was finished in 1888, nine years after work started. The book contains a line of thanks to 'Dr W. C. Minor'.

They did not, of course, know that Dr W. C. Minor was as mad at that time as when he had first entered Broadmoor. His guards and doctors had noticed that Minor's condition had improved when he first started work on the dictionary. But as the years went on, the years between the ages of fifty and sixty for Minor, the old problems returned.

In September 1884 he wrote to Dr Orange that someone was coming into his cell and writing on his books. He wrote that his cell door had opened at 3 a.m. the night before. If nothing was done, he wrote, 'I shall have to send my books back to London and have them sold.'

A few months later Minor feared that the people who were coming into his cell at night would start a fire. Later he complained that the night-visitors were stealing his food and his musical instruments. He said that two of the guards, named James and Annett, were making him walk about at night. He said that people from the village were coming into his cell at night. He said that people were hitting him, putting electricity through his body.

In 1896 Queen Victoria said that the next book of the dictionary, C, could have her name on the front page. This was, of course, a great honour and meant that the dictionary was at last a success. At about the same time, one of the dictionary's best contributors was insane and writing that a guard by the name of Coles had come into his cell at night and 'used my body'.

Chapter 9 Dr Murray's Work on the *OED*

James Murray was very unhappy in the early years of his work on the dictionary and nearly gave up the work on several occasions. The Delegates at Oxford University Press were more involved in the everyday work of dictionary-making than he wanted, and he thought they were not giving him enough money. The work was taking much longer than he had expected, and his health was poor from the long hours he spent working on the dictionary.

But the Delegates had told him to publish small parts of the dictionary as soon as they were ready, to earn money, and the first of these was published on 29 January 1884. It was a cheap-looking book that had entries for some, but not all, the words beginning with *A*. This was five years after Murray had started as editor and twenty-seven years after Chenevix Trench's lecture to the Philological Society.

Murray was proud, and all the many problems of making an enormous dictionary seemed to disappear when he held the little published part of a dictionary in his hand. So, feeling optimistic the day before his forty-seventh birthday, he told the world that the complete dictionary would be published in another eleven years. It took another forty-four years.

But at least people in England and America (where the dictionary part was on sale in New York for three dollars and twenty-five cents) could see the wonderful book that was slowly being created.

The first word in the first part was the letter *a*, which had four pages of entries. Then came a word that does not exist now, but in 1430 the word *aa* meant a stream. There was, of course, a quotation to prove this. Then there was a plant called an *aal*.

More usual words have their entries too, of course. There are entries for *animal* and *answer* in the first 350 pages of a book that eventually, forty years later, had 15,487 pages.

Six months after the first part was published, James and Ada Murray and their nine children moved to a new office in Oxford. Murray stopped teaching at Mill Hill School and worked full time on the dictionary. He worked hard, long hours for very little money.

The Murrays lived in a large house in the north of Oxford, at 78 Banbury Road. The house was called Sunnyside. It was large and comfortable and was the sort of house the Delegates themselves might live in.

Murray's new office for working on the dictionary was put up in the back garden. The neighbours did not like a large office in the next garden, so Murray made it lower in the ground. This made it wet and cold to work in and also produced a hill of earth which the neighbours did not like either.

The editors who worked in the office did not like it because it was so uncomfortable, but it was a lot bigger than the Mill Hill office, which still exists, next to the library at the school. The new office also had a lot more space for the slips of paper: there were shelves all round the office for them. There were long tables in the middle of the office, where the editors could work. Murray's chair was higher than his assistants' (at Mill Hill his desk had been higher too), so he could look down on all the work of editing.

Slips came in by post every morning. One editor checked each quotation quickly to see that it was complete and all the words were spelled properly; then a second editor put the new slips into alphabetical order. This second editor was often one of Murray's children, who were employed as soon as they could read, and paid sixpence a week for half an hour a day. A third editor then divided the entries into nouns, verbs and other parts of speech and then a fourth editor put the quotations for each entry in time order, starting with the earliest.

The meanings of each word were separated, following all the meanings the word had from its first use until that time. Then an editor wrote a suggested definition of the word – the most important part of most dictionaries – for Murray to check later.

It is not easy to write good definitions of words. There are rules. A noun must first be defined by the group that it belongs to (a chair belongs in the group 'furniture'). And then the differences between the word and other members of the group must be explained (a chair is used to sit on). There must be no words in the definition that are more difficult than the word which is being defined, or less likely to be known. All the words in the definition must be defined on other pages of the dictionary; it cannot be possible for a user of the dictionary to find a word in a definition that cannot be found as another entry. Also the definitions must be simple and not too long.

After the definitions had been written, all the meanings for each entry were arranged from the first to the most recent. Then the user of the dictionary could see from the definitions, as well as from the quotations, how the meaning of the word had changed with time.

If there was any more work to do after this, it was done by Murray himself. Murray added the information about which language the word originally came from and how the word should be pronounced. This is an area that always causes problems, as people argue about which pronunciation is correct.

Murray then chose the best quotations. If possible, he wanted at least one sentence from the literature of each century in which the word was used – unless it was a very fast-changing word and needed more quotations to show the changes of meaning.

Murray looked at the editor's suggested definition and wrote the definition that went into the dictionary. The page was then printed in Oxford, in Walton Street, not far from Worcester College.

Murray's letters tell us a lot about the difficulties. It was hard to make a dictionary. It was also hard to make sure that the publishers got back some of the money that they were paying in wages and costs all the time. The publishers hoped that two parts – 600 pages of finished dictionary – could be published each year. Murray tried to complete work on thirty-three words every day, but he often found that one word took him nearly a whole day.

Murray spoke about the difficulties of his work in a lecture to the Philological Society and wrote about them in the *Athenaeum* magazine. He wrote that dictionary-making was like going through a forest where nobody had ever been before. He wrote that there could be twenty or thirty or forty suggested definitions for a word like *above*. The editor had to put them all on the floor and move them about. It was like playing a board game, trying to see how the word had changed with time. He wrote that at other times it seemed impossible to define a word. He gave the word *art* as an example of this.

Murray did not say so in his report, but he solved the problem of the word *art* by sending it to Dr Minor. It was the first time that the dictionary-makers at Oxford had written to Broadmoor asking for help with a special word – though they did this many times afterwards.

The word *art* shows the problems that the dictionary-makers had. When they wrote to Dr Minor, they had already found sixteen different meanings for the noun, but they were sure there were more. Did Dr Minor, they asked politely, have any references for the word *art*?

Murray received eighteen letters offering help about the word *art* – most of them from people who had read about his work in the *Athenaeum*. But the most useful reply came from Broadmoor. Most readers sent in a sentence or two about the word *art*. Dr Minor had found twenty-seven quotations, most of them from *Discourses,* written by Sir Joshua Reynolds in 1769.

It was clear to the dictionary-makers that this Dr Minor was not only very careful in his work but also produced a lot of quotations and could find a lot of books. They were very pleased.

The correspondence about the word *art* was the start of a relationship between Murray and Minor that lasted until death separated them thirty years later. This relationship, based on work for the dictionary, was stronger than ordinary friendship.

Chapter 10   The Friendship Between Murray and Minor

Hayden Church's story of the first time Murray and Minor met, which he wrote in *Strand* magazine in September 1915, was told again and again all over England. It helped people to forget the 1914–18 war. The year 1915 was the time of the second battle of Ypres, of the defeat at Gallipoli, of the sinking of the *Lusitania,* and the story of Murray and Minor was a welcome change from bad news.

Whenever the story of the making of the dictionary was told after 1915, Church's story of Murray and Minor's first meeting was repeated. Murray's granddaughter, K. M. Elizabeth Murray, uses Church's story in her excellent book about her grandfather. The story appears again in a book about the history of dictionary-making, written by Jonathon Green in 1996. An

Oxford University Press editor, Elizabeth Knowles, who became interested in the story in the 1990s, has doubts about it and she is clearly surprised that nobody really knows anything about Murray and Minor's first meeting. Church's story is so pleasant and has been repeated so often that it has been accepted as the truth.

But the truth is also a pleasant and romantic story. It is told in a letter Murray wrote to a friend, Dr Francis Brown, in Boston. The letter was found in a wooden box in the home of one of Minor's relatives, who is now retired and living in Riverside, Connecticut. The letter does not seem to be a copy, although many letter writers of that time wrote and kept copies of every letter they sent.

His first contact with Minor, Murray wrote, came very soon after the beginning of his work on the dictionary – probably in 1880 or 1881. Murray wrote that Minor was a very good contributor who wrote to him often. Murray thought he was a doctor working at Broadmoor who had plenty of free time.

The two men wrote only about work on the dictionary. Murray was grateful to Minor for all his help, and surprised at some of the rare and expensive old books that he had in his library.

Murray and Minor wrote to each other for many years. Then one day, some time between 1887 and 1890, Mr Justin Winsor, who was visiting Murray from the Harvard College Library, thanked Murray for mentioning Minor's name among the people he thanked at the front of the dictionary. Justin Winsor then told Murray the story of Minor's life.

Murray, of course, was surprised by the story. But Minor had never mentioned anything about himself, so Murray did not think that he should tell Minor that he knew about the asylum and the murder. He also did not want their relationship to change, so he just wrote to Minor more kindly than before, but still only about the dictionary.

Then an American visitor (Murray could not remember his name) told Murray that he had visited Minor at Crowthorne. Minor, said the American visitor, had no doubt that Murray knew about the murder. And Minor would enjoy a visit from Murray. Dr Orange had left Crowthorne by this time, so Murray wrote to the new governor, Dr Nicholson.

Dr Nicholson was very happy for Murray to come to Crowthorne and visit Minor. In January 1891, the asylum governor met Murray at the railway station and took him by coach to Broadmoor. Both Murray and Minor were probably surprised when they first saw each other, because they looked so similar.

Both were tall and thin and did not have very much hair on the top of their heads. But they both had white beards and moustaches. Both of them had deep, very blue eyes. Neither of them wore glasses (though Minor needed them). Murray's nose was slightly straighter. They probably seemed like kind old uncles to Nicholson's children, who were there at the first lunch with their father.

As well as letting Minor play with his children, Dr Nicholson helped him in many ways. He let Minor order books from London, New York and Boston. He could write to anybody and the letters were not read before they were sent. He could have visitors whenever he wanted and he later told Murray that Eliza Merrett, who he thought was an attractive woman, was allowed to come to his rooms.

Minor was also allowed magazines, like the *Spectator* which was sent from London, or *Outlook*, which was posted to him by his family in Connecticut. There was also the *Athenaeum* as well as *Notes and Queries*, a strange little magazine from Oxford, which – then and now – is about mysteries in the world of books.

Before and after that first lunch with Nicholson and his family, Murray sat with Minor in his cell. He thought Minor was an excellent scholar and a moral man, who accepted his sad life in an asylum.

Murray learned (probably from the governor) that Minor gave a lot of the money he still received from the American government to Eliza Merrett. Dr Nicholson had a very high opinion of Minor and often took visitors to the asylum to Minor's cell to meet him. He also helped Minor in any way he could.

After that first meeting Murray and Minor met regularly for more than twenty years. They respected each other, they both had a love of words and eventually they became friends. They liked each other, and Murray understood Minor's moods. He contacted Nicholson before each meeting with Minor, and if the patient was unhappy and angry with the world, Murray stayed in Oxford. If Minor was unhappy but could still be helped, Murray caught the train and went to Crowthorne.

When the weather was bad, the two men sat together in Minor's cell, which looked like an Oxford student's room or like the room that Balliol College, Oxford, later gave to Murray. They sat opposite shelves of rare books – many from the sixteenth and seventeenth century – which Minor was using for his dictionary work. There was a fire which kept them warm while they talked. Tea and cake were brought in by another patient, who worked for Minor – something allowed by Dr Nicholson.

The two men talked mainly about words; usually about individual words, but sometimes about general problems of the way words were used or pronounced in different areas. But they also definitely discussed Minor's illness. Murray noticed, for example, that there was a sheet of metal on the floor to stop men coming into the cell through the floor at night. And there was a bowl of water at the door to keep evil spirits away. Murray knew about Minor's fears that someone would take him away from his cell at night, make him have sex and then take him back to the cell in the morning.

When the first aeroplanes flew in America, Minor was very interested in them and brought them into his terrible fears. He feared that someone would come into his cell, take him by aeroplane to Constantinople and make him have sex with bad women and small girls. It was difficult for Murray to listen to these terrible stories, but he said nothing. He felt sad, but he liked Minor and he also needed his work for the dictionary.

When the weather was fine, the two men walked together along paths in the gardens of the asylum. Watched by the guards, they walked past other patients walking, playing football or just sitting on one of the wooden seats and doing nothing.

They walked with their hands behind their backs, talking all the time, sometimes showing each other books or papers. They never talked to the other patients and seemed to be in a world of their own.

Sometimes Dr Nicholson invited them for afternoon tea. Sometimes Ada Murray went with her husband to Broadmoor and stayed with the Nicholson family in their comfortable house, while her husband and William Minor talked in Minor's cell or walked in the gardens.

Minor was always sad when it was time for the editor to leave. The gates shut behind him, leaving Minor alone again. Then he took down another book from his shelves, chose a word and worked until he could send his work by post to *Dr Murray, Oxford*. The post office at Oxford knew Dr Murray and his work so well that no street name or number was needed.

Whenever Minor wrote to Murray, the letters showed independence about some matters but dependence about others. As a dictionary reader and contributor he was independent, but he also desperately wanted to know that he was being helpful. He wanted praise. He wanted to be part of the group that was making the dictionary. He wanted his cell to be a different room where dictionary-making was done, just as it was done in

Oxford. He also wanted everybody at the asylum to know that he was different from the others in their cells.

Even before he had met Minor, Murray seemed to understand him from the letters. He immediately noticed that Minor preferred to work on words that the dictionary-makers needed at that time. Words that would not be published for years did not interest him.

Murray often talked about his friend and mentioned him (and his problem) when he lectured about making the dictionary. In 1897, for example, Murray lectured at a Dictionary Evening at the Philological Society. He said he had received fifteen or sixteen thousand slips during the past year. Half of these came from Dr W. C. Minor, whose sad story, Murray said, was known to his audience. Dr Minor had been reading fifty or sixty unusual books from the sixteenth and seventeenth centuries. He was always just a little ahead of work on the dictionary.

Two years later Murray told his lecture audience even more about Dr Minor. The most important contributor, he told his audience, was Dr W. C. Minor of Broadmoor, who during the past two years had sent in no fewer than 12,000 quotations. These were nearly all for the words that the dictionary needed at that time because Dr Minor liked 'to feel that he is in touch with the making of the dictionary'. Murray then said that Minor's help over the last seventeen or eighteen years had been 'so enormous' that his quotations would show words over four centuries.

Chapter 11   The Later Years of Dr Minor

Even today people ask why William Chester Minor did not attend the Great Dictionary Dinner on Tuesday 13 October 1897. The dinner was in Oxford and Minor was invited.

The whole country celebrated in 1897: Queen Victoria had

been Queen of England for sixty years. Oxford was also in the mood for a party because by then the dictionary was going well. After the slow progress of the early years, it was being published much more quickly. The dictionary part *Anta* to *Battening* had been published in 1885, *Battenlie* to *Bozzom* in 1887, *Bra* to *Byzen* in 1888. The dictionary-makers were working efficiently and confidently. There was no doubt now that the dictionary would one day be finished.

So Oxford University gave a big dinner to honour and thank James Murray. The dinner was at Queen's College, Oxford. The *Times* wrote about it, praising the dictionary as one of the greatest of the university's achievements. The dinner itself was a famous event in the history of Oxford. Guests sat at long tables, ate excellent English food and drank excellent French wine.

Fourteen people made speeches at the dinner. Murray talked about the history of dictionary-making; someone from Oxford University Press spoke about the dictionary's importance to England; and Furnivall continued his interest in women by making a speech about why more of them should be allowed to study at the university.

All of England's important scholars were there, as well as all the editors of the dictionary, the Delegates, members of the Philological Society and many of the contributors. But a lot of these people were discussing two contributors who were not there. The two were similar in many ways: both were American, both spent time in India, both were soldiers, both were mad – and although both were invited to that dinner, neither of them came.

The other American was Dr Fitzedward Hall, who came from Troy, New York. His life was a strange story. He was going to study at Harvard University in 1848, but his family sent him to Calcutta to find his brother and bring him back home. His ship sank, but he was rescued and stayed in India to study the Sanskrit language.

He learned Sanskrit so well that he was offered a job lecturing in Sanskrit at Government College in Benares. Then he fought in the British army and left India in 1860 to lecture in Sanskrit at King's College, London.

He left his job after a quarrel with another Sanskrit scholar, called Theodore Goldstücker. He left the Philological Society at the same time and went to live in a small village in the country, in Marlesford, Suffolk.

People in Marlesford said that he drank too much, that he was a spy, that he was not really a scholar and that he did not lead a moral life. He said that the people in Marlesford had made life impossible for his wife, so she had to leave the village. He said that they hated Americans and that they had ruined his life. He locked himself into his little house in the village and, except for occasional holidays in New York, never went anywhere.

But he wrote to Murray at Oxford every day, and they wrote to each other for twenty years. The two men never met – but over the years Hall wrote slips for the dictionary, answered questions, offered advice and was always a good friend to the dictionary in its most difficult times.

Murray thanked Hall at the front of the dictionary, where all the thanks, including those to Minor, were written. He thanked Hall for his help with more words than he could count. Hall's work, wrote Murray, could be found 'on every page'.

Many people at the dinner knew that Dr Fitzedward Hall did not usually leave his house and so nobody was surprised that he was not at the dinner. But there were some who expected Dr Minor.

But sadly the last two years had not been good to Minor. His kind friend Dr Nicholson, the governor of Broadmoor, had retired in 1895. Six years earlier a patient had attacked Dr Nicholson – he had hit him on the head – and the governor was still in pain. His idea of letting patients like Minor have a fairly easy life was now not popular. The new governor, Dr Brayn, thought that an asylum should be more like a prison.

Dr Brayn thought of himself as a prison guard, and he was a good one. Nobody escaped from Broadmoor while he was governor. The patients were locked in their cells alone. They feared and hated him, and Murray thought he was treating Minor badly.

Minor was very unhappy. He said that he had been wearing somebody else's shoes at night, and now his socks had holes in them (November 1896). He thought someone was putting something in his wine that should not be there.

Then Dr Brayn was warned in a letter that two of Minor's family had recently killed themselves. Minor might do the same thing, the letter said, if it was a family problem. But the information did not make Minor's life at Broadmoor worse: the governor took no action against him.

A few years earlier Minor had asked for a pocket-knife. Some of the books he bought from booksellers in London and America did not have their pages cut and he needed to cut the pages. Even in Dr Brayn's time, he was allowed to keep the knife.

But he started walking in the garden even in very bad weather. If he wanted to walk outside in a snowstorm, he shouted that he would and nobody was going to stop him. Again, even in Brayn's time, he was allowed to do this.

Some of Minor's army friends were in London in 1899, and they all asked to come to Broadmoor to see him. But Minor refused to see them, saying that he did not know their names.

He asked to leave Broadmoor for a short time but to stay in the area, which some patients at that time were allowed to do. The answer to this was a definite 'No'. Dr Brayn wrote that he did not think that this would be a good idea. On the back of the letter the cold Dr Brayn wrote, 'Patient informed, 12.12.89. R. B.'

The letter was the first in Minor's file that was typed. As

Minor grew older in Broadmoor, the world was changing around him and the typewriter had been invented.

At this time Minor was not eating well. He was eating some heavy food, but not very much meat. He was more and more unhappy, and had no energy.

A visit from Murray in the summer of 1901 made him feel a little happier for a short time, but soon the editors at the dictionary noticed that their contributor was a changed man. 'I notice that he has sent no Q quotations,' wrote Murray to a friend. But for some months, the letter continued, he had done very little and little had been heard from him. Minor, of course, always did less in summer because he spent more time outside, walking in the gardens. But in the summer of 1901 he had done less than usual. Murray was talking about going to see him, to get him interested in the dictionary again, which had certainly not been necessary earlier. Murray at this time thought of Minor as a lonely and sad man. His visits to Broadmoor were to encourage him to continue his work.

A month after Murray wrote that to a friend, things were no better. They were worse. There were stories of Minor 'refusing to do the work that was wanted'. At about the time Queen Victoria died (1901) Murray noted one word that Minor had provided quotations for, and that was all.

In March 1902 another of Minor's old army friends wrote to Brayn, asking if he could visit Minor. He wrote that he had written to Minor and Minor had replied, telling him not to come. Minor had written that Broadmoor was now a very different place and that his army friend 'might find it unpleasant'. The friend asked Brayn for advice, adding that he did not want his wife to see anything unpleasant.

Brayn agreed that the old army friend should not come: 'I do not think it would be advisable for you to visit.' Brayn said that he did not think Minor was in 'immediate danger', but that Minor was getting old and might not live much longer.

Minor was clearly not the man he had been even a few years ago, and about this time came the first suggestion that he should spend the end of his life in America, close to his family.

By this time Minor had been in Broadmoor for thirty years – longer than any other patient. He lived for his books and he was deeply sad. He missed the kind and sympathetic Dr Nicholson; he did not understand the hard life that Dr Brayn had created for the patients in Broadmoor. There had been only one other patient clever enough for Minor to talk to, and that was the strange painter Richard Dadd, who had been sent to Broadmoor for killing his own father with a knife. But Dadd was dead by this time.

Judith Minor, too, was dead. He had seen her in 1885, when she visited Broadmoor on her way back from India. But she had died in New Haven in 1900. Many of the people that the mad old man knew were now gone.

Even old Fitzedward Hall had died, in 1901. Minor had written a long, sad letter about it to Murray. In the letter he asked Murray to send some slips for the letters K and O. It seems that the death of Hall reminded Minor of his work. But only a little. He was now quite alone. His health was getting worse. He was no danger to anyone, except himself. He was sixty-seven years old and it showed in his face. He was an old man in an asylum and his life was becoming harder and harder to live.

Dr Francis Brown wanted to help. This was the doctor in Boston who Murray had written to, telling him about his first meeting with Minor. When he heard from Murray again, Brown wrote to the army in Washington and then to the American government and then, in March 1902, to Dr Brayn.

He suggested that a letter was sent to the British government, requesting that Minor was returned to his family in America. His family, wrote Dr Brown, would be happy for Minor to 'spend his last days in his own land and nearer to them.' Dr Brown also suggested that it would not be a good idea to tell Minor about this until there was definite news.

But Brayn did not help Dr Brown. He showed no pity for the old man who was his patient. The American army and government also did nothing. The old man had to stay, helped a little by letters from Murray in Oxford, but mainly angry and sad.

But his life was going to get even worse. Something terrible was going to happen to William Minor. Something that the journalist Hayden Church called the main event of Minor's sad life. It happened on a cold morning at the beginning of December 1902.

Chapter 12   A Terrible Event

'At 10.55 a.m. Dr Minor came to the ... gate, which was locked, and he called out: "You had better send for the Medical Officer at once! I have injured myself!" '

The words are the first lines in a note in pencil in the file on the daily life of Broadmoor Patient Number 742. The file is full of reports about the details of William Minor's life alone in Broadmoor. It lists what he ate; it names the smaller and smaller number of visitors he had; it records the old man getting weaker, his anger, his insane stories about what had happened to him. Usually these reports are written in steady, confident and neat handwriting.

But this note, which is dated 3 December 1902, is very different. The first difference is that it is written in thick pencil. But the handwriting, too, is different. It seems that the man who wrote this note was frightened, or perhaps out of breath, or in shock.

The note was written by one of the guards for Block 2, Mr Coleman. If he was in shock when he wrote the note, he had a

66

good reason. The note continues that Coleman sent another guard, Harfield, to get the Medical Officer and then he tried to help Dr Minor. Then Dr Minor told Coleman what he had done. He had cut his penis off. Minor said he had tied it with string, to stop the bleeding, and Coleman looked and saw that that was what he had done.

Dr Baker and Dr Nott then saw him, reported Coleman, and Minor was taken to the hospital in Block B3 at 11.30 a.m.

'He had taken his walk before breakfast as usual. Also he took his breakfast. I was talking to him at 9.50 . . . when he appeared to be just as usual.'

But he was not 'just as usual' – whatever that phrase might mean for a man like Minor, who believed that men visited him at night and took him away. It is, of course, possible that Minor's terrible action was caused by an equally terrible event that had just happened, though there is no proof of that. But it is more likely that Minor had been planning this for several days at least, and perhaps for months.

In Minor's mind it was necessary for him to cut off his penis, so that he could forgive himself. His doctors believed that he had become more religious two years before, at the end of the century, thirty years after he had been sent to Broadmoor.

He was the son of very religious parents, and in his early years he was a member of the Congregationalist Church. But during his time at Yale he had stopped going to church, and by the time he was in the army he had given up his religion completely. This was perhaps because of the terrible events he saw in battle, or perhaps he simply lost interest in going to church.

But whatever the reason, after his time in the army he described himself as someone who did not believe in God. The laws of nature, he wrote, could explain everything that happened on earth, so there was no need for God to exist. Like many people at this time, Minor read the books of T. H. Huxley;

Huxley's philosophy was that God may or may not exist – we do not know. Minor thought we could be certain: for Minor, God did not exist.

But slowly, over the years spent in the asylum, Minor's feelings of anger at the idea of God began to grow weaker. By about 1898 his certainty that there was no God was not total. Perhaps this was because of his regular talks with James Murray, who was a very religious man and someone who Minor liked and admired. Did Murray discuss religion with Minor? Perhaps he encouraged Minor to find calm and peace inside himself by accepting the idea of God. If he did, powerful religious feelings perhaps grew in Minor.

By 1900 Minor had changed. He was telling visitors, and even writing to the Broadmoor governor, that he now believed in God, although he was not a member of any religious group. It was an important decision – but it was also a tragic one.

It was tragic because Minor began to judge himself in the way he thought God was judging him. He stopped thinking of his insanity as something that was sad but that he could improve. Instead, he starting thinking of it as something that he could not live with, something against God that he had to punish himself for. In his own eyes he was not a sad man who people should pity; he was a terrible man, not completely human.

He had always masturbated very often, but now he believed that God would punish him for it and for depending on it so much. He had always thought about sex, but now he hated himself for it. His memories – real or imaginary – of women he had had sex with returned to him and filled him with hate for himself. He began to hate the body that God had given him.

According to his medical file, Minor believed that he had had sex with thousands of women, night after night for more than twenty years. The file also said that masturbation had made his penis larger, that a French woman had admired his penis, and that sex and the thought of sex had given him great pleasure. But, the file added, when he became religious he realized that he could end this life of sex by cutting off his penis.

There is one other possible reason for this amazing act. It is almost unbelievable, but it should at least be mentioned. He possibly cut off his penis because of his guilt at a relationship with the widow of the man he had murdered – or because he wished for or dreamt about a relationship with her.

Eliza Merrett had visited Minor regularly in his cell at the asylum in the early 1880s. She used to bring books and occasional presents. Minor and Judith Minor had given her money after the loss of her husband. Eliza Merrett had said, in public, that she forgave Minor for the murder. She accepted, sympathetically, that he had killed her husband at a moment when he did not know right from wrong.

She and Minor were the same age, and in many ways similarly unhappy people. Was it completely impossible that while they tried to make each other a little happier, something happened between them? And was it perhaps, many years later, the memory of this that sent the thoughtful and sensitive Minor into the state of guilt from which he found such a terrible way out?

Nobody has ever suggested that the meetings between Minor and Eliza were wrong in any way. But it is also possible that Minor's guilt came from the pictures of her in his mind and from imagined events, not from what actually happened when they met.

So it is possible, but only possible, that guilt for a real or imaginary action caused Minor to do what he did, and not the slow growth of his religious feelings.

♦

It is so dangerous to remove a man's penis that doctors very rarely do it. There is a very small, blood-drinking fish in Brazil which can get inside a man. The fish cannot be removed except by cutting off the penis. This is the only time that doctors will remove it. Any man who operates on himself in this way is very brave, but he is doing something that is desperate and dangerous. It is even more desperate and dangerous when the man uses an ordinary knife and operates on himself in an ordinary room, not in a clean hospital.

Some years earlier Minor had asked for the knife to cut the pages of new books, but he had not used it for a long time. He kept the knife in his pocket for whenever he needed it, and now his need was unusual and urgent and terrible. He was a doctor, of course, and he knew how to operate on a patient.

So that Wednesday morning he made the knife as sharp as he could, using a stone. He tied a thin piece of string round the end of his penis to stop some of the bleeding after he had cut it off. He waited about ten minutes, also to make sure that there was less bleeding. Then, in one quick cut, he removed his penis, leaving about thirty millimetres of it still on his body.

He threw his penis into the fire in his room. He untied the string. As he had expected, there was almost no blood. He lay on his bed for a time, until he was sure that there was no sudden bleeding – and then he walked without hurrying to the nearest guard in Block 2. He knew, as a doctor, that his body would go into shock and that he would need to go to the hospital – which is where the amazed Broadmoor doctors sent him.

He was in hospital for almost a month. But within days he was the same angry William Chester Minor, complaining about the noise that workmen were making – although the day he complained was a Sunday, and the workmen were all at home.

Minor's penis recovered from what he had done to it. He could still use it to go to the toilet, but not for any sexual purpose. This, of course, was what he wanted. His problem was now solved. He had shown God that there could be no more sex.

Minor's doctor, in his notes about his patient, wrote that his courage was amazing.

◆

Exactly a year later, the idea of sending Minor back to America was suggested again. Minor's brother Alfred, still running his shop in New Haven, suggested it to the governor in a letter that Minor never saw. This time, for the first time, Dr Brayn gave the Minor family some hope. He wrote that the American government would have to agree to the idea, and there would have to be medical care for Minor in America. But if all that could be arranged, it was 'quite possible' that Minor could leave Broadmoor.

A year after that Murray visited Minor on the way back home from a visit to his daughter at college in London. He told Brayn that Minor was 'my friend', and said later how weak Minor looked. It was sad, said Murray, how the energy Minor had had in his dictionary-making days of ten years ago was now gone. Murray, too, wanted Minor to be allowed to go home to die. In England he had no family and no work, no reason to live. His life had become a slow tragedy, as he died in front of everyone's eyes.

Minor was pleased to see Murray again and showed his pleasure like a true friend: later he gave Murray a small amount of money. Murray was going to Cape Colony, now South Africa, to lecture, and somehow Minor found out that Murray had only just enough money for the journey (although the Oxford University Press Delegates gave him a hundred pounds). So Minor sent a few pounds too, and a very friendly note. In the note he said that even a very rich man can use another pound or two.

During the next few weeks the insane man also became a very weak and ill man. He fell in the bath, he hurt his leg, he fell again and he suffered in the cold weather and caught a cough. Old age is a difficult enough time for the sane, but Minor had all the pain in his mind to live with, as well as the pain in his body.

He was also still angry, fighting his unequal fights with Dr Brayn. He was not a dictionary-maker now, and he had stopped playing his musical instruments, but Minor still painted and spent many hours in his cell with his paints.

One day he had an idea: he wanted to send one of his better paintings to the Princess of Wales. This was the young woman – her name was Mary of Teck – who was the wife of the future king, George V.

Dr Brayn said no. There was a rule at Broadmoor which said that no patient could correspond with any member of the Royal Family. This was because so many patients at Broadmoor thought they *were* members of the Royal Family. Dr Brayn, of course, was not a man who would break a Broadmoor rule to help a patient. He told Minor he could not send the painting.

Dr Minor was angry and wrote a formal letter to the British government, asking for permission to send the picture. This forced Brayn to write formally to the government with his reasons for saying no, and he also sent the picture. The government, not surprisingly, supported Brayn. Brayn wrote again to Minor, telling him that he could not send the painting.

This made Minor even angrier. He wrote a letter to the American government, asking them to send the painting to the Princess of Wales for him. Minor wanted to send the painting with the letter, but Brayn did not allow it. Minor then wrote to the United States army in Washington saying that he, an army officer, was being prevented from writing to his own government.

Letters were written and sent all summer by officials in London and Washington, all discussing whether this mad old man's rather nice painting could go to the Princess of Wales or not.

But it never did. The answer was no from the officials – and the story had an even sadder end for Minor. He wrote again, asking only for the return of his painting. The handwriting in the letter is shaky and unsteady. He was told coldly that the painting had been lost. It was never found.

There was even more unhappiness on the way for Minor. History will probably not judge Dr Brayn kindly for his treatment of William Chester Minor. In early March 1910 he took all Minor's extra comforts away. Minor was told that the next day he would have to leave the two rooms where he had lived for nearly thirty-eight years. He would not have his books with him. He could not use a writing desk or have his paints with him, or his musical instruments. He had to live in the Broadmoor hospital.

It was a cruel act of revenge by Brayn, and angry letters were sent to Broadmoor from Minor's few remaining friends. There was even a letter from Ada Murray, complaining about the way the 75-year-old Minor was being treated. Brayn replied that Minor had been moved because of 'the risk of a serious accident' – which nobody believed.

James and Ada Murray now tried everything possible to have their scholar friend sent home to America, away from the terrible Dr Brayn and an asylum that was now a cruel prison, not a kind home to dictionary-making.

Alfred Minor sailed to London in late March to try to find a solution. He had spoken to the US army in Washington; the army said it was possible for Minor to come home if the British government agreed. Minor could go back to the asylum where he had lived so many years before – the Government Hospital for the Insane in Washington. It was thought that if Alfred Minor looked after his brother on the journey back to America, the British government might agree.

Finally, at the end of his life, Minor had a little luck. The member of the British government who made the decision about him was Winston Churchill (who was later better known than he was then). Churchill's mother was American, and he was always sympathetic to Americans. He asked for the details of Minor's situation.

His officials listed reasons for sending Minor back to America and reasons against. The decision was then made according to whether Minor was still a danger to others, and whether his brother Alfred could keep him away from guns on the journey back to America. The officials decided that Minor was not dangerous, and that he should be allowed to go home.

On Wednesday 6 April 1910 Winston S. Churchill signed, in blue ink, permission for Minor to leave the United Kingdom. Minor was also told that he must not come back.

The next day James Murray wrote to Brayn, asking if he and Ada Murray could visit Broadmoor and say goodbye to Minor. Brayn wrote that there would be no problem: '... he is in much better health and will be pleased to see you.' It is easy to imagine that the old man was a little happier at the thought that after thirty-eight years he was finally going home.

Murray invited a professional photographer to take a photograph of his old friend and contributor before he left England. The photograph is a sympathetic picture of a kind, happy old scholar having tea in an English garden, with no troubles on his mind.

Early in the morning of Saturday 16 April 1910 a guard called Spanholtz took Minor to London. James and Ada Murray were at Broadmoor to say goodbye to him, and both had tears in their eyes. There was also a short goodbye from Dr Brayn.

By this time the first six books of the *New English Dictionary*, as the *OED* was still called, were finished. The dictionary was nearly half-written, and all six big books were in Minor's suitcase.

Two hours later Minor and Spanholtz were at Bracknell Railway Station. From there they travelled to Waterloo Station; only a few hundred metres away, Minor had murdered George

Merrett in 1872. Now they took a coach to St Pancras and a boat train to Tilbury Docks, where the *SS Minnetonka* was waiting to take Minor to New York.

There, in front of the ship, stood Alfred Minor, who signed a receipt for his brother before the guard left for the return journey to Broadmoor. The receipt said that William Chester Minor 'has ... been received from the Broadmoor ... Asylum into my care'. It was signed 'Alfred W. Minor'.

At two o'clock the ship left Tilbury Docks and sailed into the River Thames. By night she was in the Channel and by the next lunchtime England was out of sight, and William Chester Minor could see only the sea that was taking him to America and home.

Two weeks later Dr Brayn received a note from New Haven. In it Alfred Minor told the governor that his brother was in the St Elizabeth's Asylum in Washington DC. He had enjoyed the journey very much, Alfred wrote, although he had walked about much in the last few days. He had not created any problems for Alfred at night – though Alfred was pleased to see New York as the ship arrived. Alfred said he hoped to meet the governor one day, and sent him his best wishes.

Chapter 13   The End of Great Men

Old Frederick Furnivall was the first of the great dictionary-makers who died, a few weeks after the *Minnetonka* took Minor back to America.

He had known he was dying since the beginning of 1910. He remained full of fun and energy to the end, still enjoying his hobby of sailing and still working on the dictionary, as he had been for fifty years.

In letters to Murray he joked about his serious illness. He wrote that dictionary men 'go gradually', and that he would 'disappear in six months'. More seriously he wrote that, 'It's a great disappointment as I wanted to see the dictionary finished before I die.' But he added that he knew now that the dictionary would be finished and 'so that's all right.'

He died, as his doctors knew he would, in July 1910, but not before he had accepted Murray's invitation to look at the enormous entry for the word *take*. 'Before it is too late,' as Murray wrote.

Murray knew that he, too, would die soon. And he was only beginning the letter *T* in the dictionary. That letter took him five years to complete, from 1908 until 1913. Then he made another optimistic guess about when the dictionary would be finished – on his eightieth birthday, 'four years from now'.

But no. The dictionary was not completed in the next four years, and James Murray did not reach the age of eighty. He became ill in the spring of 1915; the treatment for his illness caused him pain, but he continued to work. In the summer of 1915 he completed the word *turndown*, and was continuing to help with difficult words.

He was photographed for the last time in the Oxford office on 10 July 1915. The editors and his daughters were around him, and behind him there were shelves of books. Murray looks calm in the photograph, but some of the other faces look tragic, perhaps knowing that it was the last photograph of him.

He died on 26 July 1915, and was buried in Oxford.

♦

Minor was now in his fifth year at the Government Hospital for the Insane in Washington DC. He was eventually told of Murray's death, nearly five thousand kilometres away in Oxford. But the day that Murray died was another of the bad days that Minor was suffering more and more frequently.

The hospital notes for that day, Monday 26 July, said that

Minor hit another patient. The other patient had only looked into his room. Minor, it seemed, had a bad temper and often tried to hit people. But he had little strength to hurt them, even if he wanted to. He was a very thin old man who bent over when he walked. He did not have any teeth or any hair, and his beard was long and white.

His mad eyes were still wild, but at the age of 81 his doctors did not think he was dangerous. He was allowed to walk outside the asylum if a guard went with him. He was not, of course, allowed to have a knife or scissors, as he had cut his penis off with his last knife.

But the wild ideas in his mind grew even worse during his years in St Elizabeth's. Even now he said he thought about little girls all the time, and he had dreams about what he did with them when he went out at night. He thought that birds were trying to take out his eyes, and that people forced food into his mouth.

Sometimes he was angry with the world, but more usually he was quiet and polite. He read and wrote a lot in his room. He did not want to spend time with the other patients very much and did not allow any of them into his room.

At St Elizabeth's, Minor's illness was given a new and more modern name. It was called *dementia praecox* and it meant that from an early age, the patient's twenties or thirties, he did not know what was real and what was not. The illness was different from *senile dementia*. Patients with *senile dementia* also did not know what was real and what was not real, but in their case it was because of the effects of old age.

These two names for insanity were first used by Emil Kraepelin in Heidelberg in 1899. Kraepelin thought that *dementia praecox* – unlike some other mental illnesses – had no physical cause. So it could not be helped by, for example, eating different food or taking medicine.

According to Kraepelin, there were three different types of *dementia praecox*. Minor's type was called *paranoiac dementia praecox*. Minor's belief that imaginary people were trying to hurt him was typical of this illness.

In Minor's time the only treatment for *paranoiac dementia praecox* was to lock the patient in an asylum. Some were locked away for only a very few years, some for ten or twenty years. Minor was in an asylum for most of his life. He was thirty-eight when he killed George Merrett. For forty-seven of the remaining forty-eight years of his life, he was in an asylum. He was never given any treatment, because the doctors at that time thought that there was none.

Today there would be possible treatments (as well as a new name for the illness – *schizophrenia*), but doctors now still do not understand the causes of this terrible illness. They still do not really know if the things Minor saw at the Battle of the Wilderness could actually *cause* a mind to stop completely connecting with real life.

Is it possible that this illness has no cause but is a part of the minds of certain unlucky people? Now, as then, nobody knows. Most doctors today believe that there are a number of causes and that some people are more sensitive to the disease than others. Many people could see a battle like the Wilderness or even brand a man, as Minor did, and not become ill. Minor was unlucky that he experienced events that were too much for *his* mind to accept and remain sane.

And he never got better. There are diseases of the mind today which are terrible for a short time, but in the end the patient recovers. Minor was not so lucky.

Perhaps there was something in the brains of all the members of the Minor family that made *schizophrenia* more likely – something they were born with. Two of his relations killed themselves, but we do not know the details. Maybe Minor's gentle nature – he was a painter, he played music, he read books – made him more sensitive to what he saw in the fields of blood of the Civil War. Perhaps he would have recovered if he had been treated more kindly at Broadmoor, especially in the later years there.

But while he was at Broadmoor, of course, he did his great and now famous work on the dictionary. In a way, those dictionary slips *were* his treatment and his medicine, though not, unfortunately, his cure. Year after year of calm, peaceful work gave him some rest from the mad pictures of women and the night-visitors in his head.

Eventually and sadly, even work on the great dictionary was not enough to stop the illness, and his mind went down and down into insanity.

But perhaps we should feel grateful that no treatment or attempt at treatment took him away from the great work, as modern treatment would almost certainly do. The pills that a patient would get today would mean no slips returned to Oxford and no quotations from rare books. He was mad and he stayed mad, but because of that the world of books and learning has gained from his work on the dictionary.

It is not a comfortable thought.

◆

By 1918 Minor's body and mind were weak. He often fell, he hurt himself, he got lost, he forgot things and he knew he was forgetting things. He stayed in bed for days at a time, with chairs against the door to keep the night-visitors out. It was forty-five years since the murder, fifty years since the first signs of madness had been noticed in him – but the night-visitors still came.

A year later he sent a small amount of money to his old university, Yale, just as he had sent money to his friend James Murray. A kind letter back from Yale said that they knew

Dr Minor's history, and so they were even more pleased to receive his gift.

In 1919 his nephew, Edward Minor, helped to have him moved to a hospital for insane old people in Hartford, Connecticut, known as the Retreat. In November 1919, in a snowstorm, Minor finally left the strange world of insane asylums.

He liked his new home and its woods and gardens by the river. His nephew wrote in the early winter of 1920 that the change had done Minor some good, but that he still could not look after himself. Also he was going blind, and for some months he had been unable to read. When books, the joy of his life, were gone there was probably little left to live for.

He died in his sleep on Friday 26 March 1920.

♦

A small gravestone in a poor area of New Haven is still there now, to remind the world of William Chester Minor. But Minor's work on the great dictionary remains too; and that is surely what the world will remember him for.

George Merrett and his family have no great work for the world to remember and, sadly, no gravestone either. Eliza Merrett was expecting a child when her husband was killed. She never really recovered from the shock of the murder, and started to drink too much. The alcohol finally killed her. There is no grave.

Two of her sons had unusual lives: George, the second oldest boy, took a gift of money from Judith Minor and went to Monaco. He won a large amount of money there and gave himself the title 'The King of Monaco'. He finally spent all the money and died without a penny in the south of France.

His younger brother, Frederick, shot himself dead in London, for reasons that have never been fully explained. Two of Minor's brothers also died by their own hand, which gives this story more than its share of sadness.

But the most important protagonist in this sad and strange story is the man who has been forgotten almost completely, since he was shot dead in the cold streets of Lambeth on that Saturday night in February 1872.

Perhaps there was a gravestone at the time of the funeral, but there is no gravestone now. Where George Merrett lies, there is only grass. And so this book is for George Merrett of Lambeth. Without his death, there would be no story to tell.

◆

The *New English Dictionary* was finished in 1927, with an entry for a word that does not exist in English any more – *zyxt*. There were twelve enormous books defining 414,825 words with 1,827,306 quotations. Only one word, *bondmaid*, was ever completely lost. Murray found it again a few years after *Battentlie–Bozzom* was published, and it appeared in a supplement which came out in 1933.

Four more supplements were published between 1972 and 1986. In 1989 a second edition of the dictionary was published as twenty rather smaller books. A third edition is being prepared.

ACTIVITIES

Chapters 1–2

Before you read

1 The book is called *The Surgeon of Crowthorne.*

   a Find the word *surgeon* in your dictionary. Is a surgeon a kind of doctor, policeman or lawyer?

   b Do you think Crowthorne is a person, a place or a hospital?

2 Answer the questions. Find the words in *italics* in your dictionary. They are all in the story.

   a If you *contribute* to a book, do you write all or part of it?

   b In the nineteenth century, which animals pulled a *coach*?

   c Does a *sane* person have a mental illness or not?

   d Are people in an *asylum* sane or insane?

   e When you *quote* someone, do you repeat their exact words or the general idea?

   f Is a *protagonist* an important or an unimportant character in a story?

   g If two people *correspond*, do they write or telephone?

   h Does a person who *edits* a book write it or check it?

   i Which drink is made in a *brewery*, beer or wine?

   j Do *prostitutes* sell their bodies or alcohol?

   k Is a *cottage* a small house or a large one?

After you read

3 Who or what is being described? Discuss what you know about these people and places.

   a 'enormous gates'

   b 'a large and complicated set of books'

   c 'the best way of explaining the different meanings of a single word'

   d 'the two main characters in the story'

   e 'a dark and dangerous place'

   f 'a fire burning through the day and night'

   g 'come from the country'

   h 'typical of workers'

i 'as warmly as a poor man could'

j 'not very British'

k 'the unmoving body'

l 'afraid of Irish people'

Chapters 3–5

Before you read

4 Write a list of questions about the lives of William Minor and James Murray that you hope will be answered in this book.

5 Find these words in your dictionary.

brigade   civil war   desert (v)   *edition   entry   fort   lecture missionary   monolingual   penicillin   publish   scholar*

Which words can be connected with:

a fighting?

b books, including dictionaries?

c universities?

d religion?

e medicine?

6 Read these sentences. What do you think the words in *italics* mean? Check in your dictionary.

a I recognise our cows because we *brand* them.

b Can you write your address on this *slip* of paper?

After you read

7 Are these statements true or false, or don't we know?

a Murray's favourite subject at school was history.

b Murray's family were poor but they were all clever.

c Murray and his first wife went to London because their baby was ill.

d By the time he was thirty, Murray had had two different jobs.

e Religion was important to Minor's family and to Murray's.

f Both Murray and Minor spoke a lot of languages.

g Minor went mad because of what he saw and did during the Battle of the Wilderness.

h The first dictionary with easy as well as hard words appeared in the eighteenth century.

i Johnson's dictionary tried to fix the meaning of words.

j No dictionary before the *OED* used quotations.

Chapters 6–8

Before you read

8 Chapter 6 is called 'The Start of the *OED*'. Guess what sort of dictionary the *OED* is. Check your answers after you have read the chapter.

I think the *OED* is a dictionary that …

a fixes/does not fix meanings.

b quotes/does not quote from books published in different centuries.

c quotes/does not quote from people's speech.

d uses/does not use readers as well as assistants to help with the entries.

e records/does not record all words.

9 Which of these words can describe:

a a book?

b a building?

block   supplement

After you read

10 Give Chenevix Trench's speech to the Philological Society. Talk about the history of dictionaries and why a new dictionary is needed. Explain the new dictionary. Say how the meanings of words will be found and why meanings should not be fixed.

11 Answer the questions.

a How did Minor find out about the new dictionary?

b Why was Minor sent to Block 2 in Broadmoor?

c How did Minor get money and what did he do with it?

d What did Murray want readers to do?

e How was Minor's method different from the other readers'?

Chapters 9–11

Before you read

12 Which of these do you think will be in Chapters 9–11?

a The first part of the dictionary is published.

b Murray stops teaching and works full time on the dictionary.

c Murray and his family move to Oxford.

d Murray thinks about leaving the dictionary.

e Murray and his wife visit Dr Minor more often.

f Minor visits Murray in Oxford.

g Minor comes to Oxford for a big formal dinner to celebrate the success of the dictionary.

h There is another contributor to the dictionary who was also in the army, is also American and is also mad.

i There is a new governor at the prison and conditions get worse for Minor.

After you read

13 Compare the three governors at Broadmoor: Dr Orange, Dr Nicholson and Dr Brayn.

14 Work with a partner. One of you is William Chester Minor and the other is James Murray. Have a conversation. Here are some ideas, but use your own ideas too:

  a the progress of the dictionary

  b work on one word, like *art*

  c the gardens at Broadmoor and the view from Minor's window

  d how Minor feels about the murder

  e the night-visitors in Minor's mind

Chapters 12–13

Before you read

15 Find these words in your dictionary. Are they about war or sex?

  masturbate   penis

After you read

16 Work with a partner or in a small group. Discuss:

  a when, in his life, Minor was 'lucky' and when he was 'unlucky'.

  b how Minor would be treated in your country today.

Writing

17 Imagine that you lived in Lambeth Marsh in the nineteenth century. Write about what it was like.

18 Write a letter from Mrs Fisher to a friend. Write about Minor's behaviour in your house and about the trial.

19 Write a letter from Murray to Minor. Thank Minor for his last slips and say what you want next. Tell him about progress on the dictionary (at any time).

20 Draw a plan of Minor's rooms in Broadmoor and describe them.

21 Write the letter from Ada Murray to Dr Brayn expressing anger that Minor's comforts have been taken away.

22 Choose a character in the book. Describe their personality and lifestyle, and give your opinion of them.

BESTSELLING
Penguin Readers

AT LEVEL 5

The Body

The Firm

Four Weddings and a Funeral

The Great Gatsby

Jane Eyre

The Pelican Brief

The Prisoner of Zenda

Rebecca

Tales from Shakespeare

Taste and Other Tales

A Time to Kill

Wuthering Heights

THE BEST WEBSITES FOR STUDENTS OF ENGLISH!

www.penguinreaders.com

Where the world of Penguin Readers comes to life

- Fully searchable on-line catalogue

- Downloadable resource materials

- First ever on-line Penguin Reader!

- New competition each month!

www.penguindossiers.com

Up-to-the-minute website providing articles for free!

- Articles about your favourite stars, blockbuster movies and big sports events!

- Written in simple English with fun activities!

NEW from Penguin Readers
Your favourite titles on Audio CD

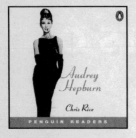
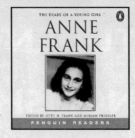
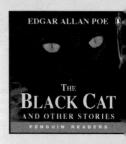

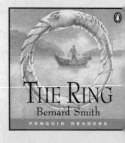

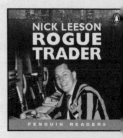